LET'S STUDY
2 CORINTHIANS

Let's Study

2 CORINTHIANS

Derek Prime

THE BANNER OF TRUTH TRUST

THE BANNER OF TRUTH TRUST
3 Murrayfield Road, Edinburgh EH12 6EL
P.O. Box 621, Carlisle, PA 17013, USA

*

© Derek Prime 2000
First Published 2000
Reprinted 2009
Reprinted 2018

ISBN: 978 0 85151 779 7

*

*

Typeset in 11/12pt Ehrhardt MT
at the Banner of Truth Trust, Edinburgh

Printed in the U.S.A by
Versa Press, Inc.,
East Peoria, IL

Contents

[vii]

Publisher's Preface

Let's Study 2 Corinthians is part of a series of books which explain and apply the message of Scripture. The series is designed to meet a specific and important need in the church. While not technical commentaries, each volume will comment on the text of a biblical book; and while not merely lists of practical applications, they are concerned with the ways in which the teaching of Scripture can affect and transform our lives today. Understanding the Bible's message and applying its teaching are the aims.

Like other volumes in the series, *Let's Study 2 Corinthians* seeks to combine explanation and application. Its concern is to be helpful to ordinary Christian people by encouraging them to understand the message of the Bible and apply it to their own lives. The reader in view is not the person who is interested in all the detailed questions which fascinate the scholar, although behind the writing of each study lies an appreciation for careful and detailed scholarship. The aim is exposition of Scripture written in the language of a friend, seated alongside you with an open Bible.

Let's Study 2 Corinthians is designed to be used in various contexts. It can be used simply as an aid for individual Bible study. Some may find it helpful to use in their devotions with husband or wife, or to read in the context of the whole family.

In order to make these studies more useful, not only for individual use but also for group study in Sunday School classes and home, church or college, study guide material will be found on pp. 135–151. Sometimes we come away frustrated rather than helped by group discussions. Frequently that is because we have been encouraged to discuss a passage of Scripture which we do not understand very well in the first place. Understanding must

[ix]

always be the foundation for enriching discussion and for thought-ful, practical application. Thus, in addition to the exposition of 2 Corinthians, the additional material provides questions to encourage personal thought and study, or to be used as discussion starters. The Group Study Guide divides the material into thirteen sections and provides direction for leading and participating in group study and discussion.

The text which forms the basis of the studies is the *English Standard Version.*

Corinth and the Corinthian Church

C orinth was the fourth largest city of the Roman empire, after Rome, Alexandria and Antioch. It had a territory of 330 square miles. The original city, one of the Greek city-states, was destroyed in 146 B.C. in a revolt against the Roman empire. The Romans plundered its Greek works of art. It was rebuilt in the time of Julius Caesar (around 46 B.C.), and resettled with freed slaves from Italy. Corinth soon regained its position of commercial importance. It was a rival of Athens, with perhaps the greatest influence in Greece.

Capital of the Roman province of Achaia and commercial bridge between East and West, Corinth was a busy commercial and mercantile centre, with Greeks, western Europeans, Syrians, Asians, Egyptians and Jews rubbing shoulders in daily business. The people built ships and manufactured articles of bronze and pottery. Its industries and position made it subject, therefore, to many outside influences. Located on the narrow isthmus of Achaia, Corinth had two harbours – one on the Aegean and the other on the Adriatic Sea. Ox carts transported goods between the two ports. Situated at such an important crossroads of the ancient world, it became notorious for its sexual vice and immorality. An ancient author went so far as to coin the verb 'to Corinthianize' for 'committing fornication'. Religious practices associated with fertility cults encouraged sexual perversion. According to tradition, which is supported by good reason (see, for instance, *Rom.* 16:23 and *1 Cor.* 1:14), Paul spent the winter of 56–57 in the city in the home of Gaius. It was there that he wrote his letter to the Romans. The description of Gentile sin in Romans 1:18–32 fits Corinth exactly.

Located on the route from Rome to the East, its key geographical position made it an ideal base for the spread of the gospel as merchants and travellers from many places passed through it.

THE BIRTH OF THE CHURCH IN CORINTH

Paul preached the gospel in Corinth in the early 50s, during his second missionary journey (*Acts* 18:1–18). An inscription from Delphi helps date the visit. It shows that Gallio came to Corinth as proconsul in A.D. 51 or 52 (*Acts* 18:12–17). Both his judgment seat and the meat market have been excavated (*1 Cor.* 10:25). When opposition grew fierce there, the Lord Jesus spoke to Paul in a vision assuring him that he had 'many in this city who are my people' (*Acts* 18:10). With this encouragement, Paul stayed on for eighteen months, 'teaching the word of God among them' (*Acts* 18:11). This longer period produced a close attachment to the Corinthians. God used Paul's ministry to establish a church in Corinth composed of both Jews and Gentiles. While there Paul wrote his letters to the Galatians and the Thessalonians. From Corinth Paul and his colleagues travelled back to Antioch by way of Jerusalem (*Acts* 18:18–22).

PAUL'S LETTERS TO THE CORINTHIANS

1 Corinthians 5:9 indicates that Paul wrote an earlier letter to the Corinthians that no longer exists. People like Chloe kept in touch with him, and the church sent him a letter requesting guidance about problems that had arisen (*e.g.*, *1 Cor.* 7:1). Stephanas, Fortunatus and Achaicus probably delivered the letter to him (*1 Cor.* 16:17). Paul later sent Timothy to visit them (*1 Cor.* 4:17; 16:10–11).

The first letter has not come down to us. Paul writes in 1 Corinthians 5:9, 'I wrote to you in my letter not to associate with sexually immoral people.' His second letter (what we know as 1 Corinthians) was sent because of reports Paul had received of party strife in Corinth (*1 Cor.* 1:11), immorality and lawsuits (*1 Cor.* 5:6), and because of the questions the Corinthians had raised.

Debate surrounds the possibility of another letter after this – but before our 2 Corinthians – known as 'the severe letter' (see *2 Cor.* 2:3, 4, 9 and 7:8, 12). Some regard 2 Corinthians 10–13 as part of this letter. We do not have sufficient evidence to arrive at a clear conclusion, but that does not influence our understanding of what Paul writes.

DISTINCTIVE FEATURES OF 2 CORINTHIANS

• It reveals the tensions in Paul's relations with the Corinthians caused by his detractors.

• It is Paul's most autobiographical letter, in which he opens his heart more than in any other.

• It is outstanding for its demonstration of the privileges and pressures of pastoral work.

• It contains unique passages about perseverance under trials, the nature of Christian service, evangelism, and giving.

• It is a neglected letter, probably because its subjects do not divide up so neatly as happens with most other New Testament books and letters.

I

God at the Centre

¹Paul, an apostle of Christ Jesus by the will of God, and Timothy our brother,
    To the church of God that is at Corinth, with all the saints who are in the whole of Achaia:
    ²Grace to you and peace from God our Father and the Lord Jesus Christ (2 Cor. 1:1–2).

If I do not recognise the handwriting when I open a letter, I look at the last page to discover the writer's identity. We do not need to do that in the New Testament, since first-century letters begin with the author's name, as here.

FUNDAMENTAL TRUTHS

Paul's opening greeting and introduction have four important truths and principles behind them. They all illustrate how God was at the centre of Paul's life. Their force is all the stronger because they are not directly stated. Essential to Paul's thinking, they came automatically to the surface.

(i) God's will determines our service and function in the church. The letter begins, 'Paul an apostle of Christ Jesus *by the will of God.*' Paul was *an apostle.* The noun comes from the verb 'to send', and means a person sent by another. The term can be used simply of messengers 'sent' by the churches, but that is not how it is used here. Such 'apostleship' is not in the same category as that of Paul and of the Twelve – the regular corporate description given to the twelve apostles Jesus appointed early in his ministry (*Mark* 6:7, *John* 6:70). They were chosen, called and sent forth by Christ himself;

they were his witnesses, especially of his resurrection. They knew in a special way the help of the Holy Spirit, who led them into all truth. God confirmed the value of their work by signs and miracles. They have no successors. (We shall consider apostleship in greater detail in chapter 17, pages 108–109.)

In particular, Paul was an apostle '*of Christ Jesus*'. The Lord Jesus Christ met him on the Damascus road and commissioned him (*Acts* 26:16–18). The whole purpose of Paul's life then became obedience to Jesus Christ. His ambition was to honour him and to see him honoured by others.

Paul was 'an apostle of Christ Jesus *by the will of God*'. God alone determines our function in the body of Christ. His will is a sovereign will. He has authority to do with his creatures as he pleases.

Paul probably begins his letter with this emphasis because some at Corinth cast doubt upon his apostleship for their own ulterior motives. From the beginning he reminds them that his position in the body of Christ, as theirs, is not a matter of self-selection but of God's choice.

(ii) The gift of spiritual life brings about our membership of God's family. Paul carefully associates Timothy with his letter to the Corinthians, for he writes, 'Timothy *our brother*'. Paul consistently identified himself with his colleagues. In recognising his special position as an apostle in the body of Christ, he did not overlook the equally important place of others.

In particular, Paul recognised Timothy to be his brother in Christ through new birth. New birth brings us into God's family. That had happened for Paul on the Damascus Road (*Acts* 9:1–9). Immediately afterwards the Lord Jesus sent a Damascus Christian called Ananias to Paul so that he might receive his sight. Ananias' first words to Paul, then called Saul, were '*Brother* Saul' (*Acts* 9:17). For Timothy, new birth came about first through the background influence of his mother and grandmother (*2 Tim.* 1:5), and then through the ministry of Paul (*2 Tim.* 1:2) as they taught him the Scriptures and pointed him to the Lord Jesus (*2 Tim.* 3:15). While Timothy recognised Paul as his spiritual father, and Paul regarded him as his spiritual son, a superior relationship was that of brother, since that extended to all the members of God's family.

(iii) God's purpose determines how we should think of the church.
Paul addresses his letter to 'the church of God that is at Corinth,
with all the saints who are in the whole of Achaia' (v. 1). Achaia was
a province of southern Greece, governed by Corinth.

The word 'church' is used in two basic ways in the Bible. It first
describes the whole body of Christ, including its members already in
heaven, as well as those on earth. It is used, secondly, to describe the
church in its local setting. The church finds geographical expression
in different places. It is a term to be used therefore either of all God's
people everywhere or of God's people in one place. The church is
made up of those, like Paul and Timothy, who have experienced the
miracle of new birth through faith in our Lord Jesus Christ.

Paul's introductory statement clearly defines the church as God's
possession. It belongs to him and is his creation. It is the fruit of his
Son's saving work. To bring the church into being, the Lord Jesus
came and died (*Eph.* 5:25–27).

Not only does the church belong to God, but it consists of those
whom God has set part for himself and whom he is sanctifying – that
is to say, it is made up of 'saints'. All Christians, though sinners,
are saints! Unfortunately, in everyday language the title is reserved
for people of particular sanctity or goodness. The Bible uses it to
describe all who know new birth and are part of the church of God.
Always used in the plural, it points to believers as a group and clearly
identifies God's purpose: his purpose is to make us holy like himself
(*1 Pet.* 1:15–16).

*(iv) Grace and peace are our greatest need and God's most appropri-
ate gifts.* 'Grace to you and peace from God our Father and the Lord
Jesus Christ' (v. 2). This greeting reminds us that our fellowship
is with the Father and the Son (*1 John* 1:3), the essence of eternal
life (*John* 17:3). God the Holy Spirit brings us into this intimate
relationship at our new birth. The Father is mentioned first because
he is the fountain of the Godhead. The Father sent the Son to be our
Saviour; the initiative in the whole plan of salvation is the Father's
(*John* 3:16, *1 John* 4:9, 10, 14).

The name 'Father' is one of the most precious words of human
language. All fatherhood and motherhood in the world at their
best derive meaning and inspiration from God's. The Bible does

[3]

not teach the universal fatherhood of God, except in the physical sense that God is the creator of all. 'Father' does not mean 'Creator' in Bible language. He is not the Father of all men and women, but of his own people, of those who through faith in his Son have become members of his family and of his Son's body, the church. God's Fatherhood of those who are in Christ may be seen as the climax of New Testament revelation. No privilege is greater than this: through Jesus we may come to the Father and call him 'Abba, Father' (*Rom.* 8:15)!

The Father and the Son delight to give the best gifts, and this prayerful greeting powerfully reminds us that grace and peace are our greatest daily need. 'Grace' originates from an Old Testament term meaning 'to bend' or 'to stoop'. It points to God's amazing condescension and kindness. His grace is His sovereign determination to bless the undeserving. Grace is synonymous with forgiveness. God's grace in his Son provides us with daily forgiveness of all our sins as we confess them to him (*1 John* 1:9). Grace is also synonymous with help and strength, freely given by God. God's grace always matches our need (*Heb.* 4:16).

Along with grace goes peace, and always in that order. Only as we know the grace of God's forgiveness may we know the renewal of his peace in our lives. Peace is well-being and includes freedom from anxiety. In relationships, peace is good will and harmony, the opposite of conflict. The wonder of God's grace in his Son is that we may be as much at peace with God as our Lord Jesus Christ himself is. As we experience his grace, we are able to pray, and to pray about everything. The exercise of prayer becomes then a path to peace of the deepest kind, a peace that passes understanding (*Phil.* 4:6–7).

God's grace and peace may be constantly renewed to us; and it is on a daily basis – moment by moment – that we require them. The more we daily enjoy God's grace and peace, the more like Paul we respond in gratitude and put God at the centre of our life. That truth may be hidden in its consequences from us, but it will be witnessed by others and hopefully conspicuously so.

2

Some of God's Purposes in Suffering

³Blessed be the God and Father of our Lord Jesus Christ, the Father of mercies and God of all comfort, ⁴who comforts us in all our affliction, so that we may be able to comfort those who are in any affliction, with the comfort with which we ourselves are comforted by God. ⁵For as we share abundantly in Christ's sufferings, so through Christ we share abundantly in comfort too. ⁶If we are afflicted, it is for your comfort and salvation; and if we are comforted, it is for your comfort, which you experience when you patiently endure the same sufferings that we suffer. ⁷Our hope for you is unshaken, for we know that as you share in our sufferings, you will also share in our comfort.

⁸For we do not want you to be ignorant, brothers, of the affliction we experienced in Asia. For we were so utterly burdened beyond our strength that we despaired of life itself. ⁹Indeed, we felt that we had received the sentence of death. But that was to make us rely not on ourselves but on God who raises the dead. ¹⁰He delivered us from such a deadly peril, and he will deliver us. On him we have set our hope that he will deliver us again. ¹¹You also must help us by prayer, so that many will give thanks on our behalf for the blessing granted us through the prayers of many (2 Cor. 1:3–11).

P aul begins his letter with an expression of praise. He praises God for the way in which he has turned hard and difficult experiences to good use. Afflictions are a common feature of life (v. 4) for Christians and non-Christians alike. The words Paul uses – 'afflictions' (vv. 4,8), 'sufferings' (vv. 5–7), '(burdens) beyond our strength'

(v. 8), 'despair' (v. 8), 'the sentence of death' (v. 9) and 'deadly peril' (v. 10) - remind us of the variety of difficulties we may meet.

NOT AN EXHAUSTIVE EXPLANATION OF SUFFERING

Paul does not attempt a comprehensive explanation of trouble and suffering, but he points to *some* purposes God may have in them. We use the word 'some' because in no sense dare we be dogmatic about God's purposes in suffering (cf. *John* 9:2–3). There is an element of mystery about it. Here and there in the Bible we get significant glimpses of what God may choose to do through our troubles, difficulties and suffering. These glimpses do not provide answers to all our questions, but they give the help and encourage-ment we need as God's children to see them through.

PURPOSE NUMBER ONE:
God comforts us so that we may be able to comfort others (vv. 3–4).

Paul's basic conviction is that God 'comforts us in all our affliction, so that we may be able to comfort those who are in any affliction, with the comfort with which we ourselves are comforted by God.' (v. 4). Essential to this conviction is the understanding Paul has, and the teaching he gives, about three aspects of God's character.

First, God is the God and Father of our Lord Jesus Christ (v. 3). There is but one God, and he is the God who sent his Son to be the Saviour (*John* 3:16). The relationship between the Father and the Son is unique: the Lord Jesus is the Father's only Son, the supreme object of his pleasure and delight. It is in his Son that the Father provides the perfect revelation of himself. Every view we have of the Father therefore needs to be totally influenced by the understanding we have of God's character in his self-revelation in his Son.

Second, God is the Father of mercies (v. 3). Mercy (or compassion) is an essential part of his character and of his self-revelation in both the Old and New Testaments (*Psa.* 116:5, *James* 5:11). It expresses God's sympathy with us in our troubles, difficulties and grief. It was wonderfully displayed in the life and character of our Lord Jesus, and it always led to appropriate action (*Matt.* 9:36; 15:32).

God's compassion arises naturally from his fatherhood (*Psa.* 103:13). Any father – like any mother – cares compassionately for

[6]

his children, particularly when they go through pain and suffering. When we call God 'Father', we are not saying that God is like us in fatherhood. Rather, we are indicating that he is the *true* Father, and that human parenthood at its best is but a reflection of his perfect parenthood.

Third, he is the God of all comfort (v. 3). As the perfect and compassionate Father, he knows and understands everything that comes to us and is able to send us the comfort we need, whatever our trouble.

The first thing we require in trouble is comfort – comfort in the sense of strength, encouragement and courage to face both the present and the future with the simple yet profound ability to live a day at a time. Our Father may choose to comfort us in all kinds of ways – hence he is the God of *all* comfort.

Comfort is something we receive *from God* (v. 4). God is the giving God (*James* 1:5). It is God's character to give us the best gifts. He makes sure that help is always on its way, even before we call upon him for it (*Isa.* 65:24). God's comfort is significantly present tense. It is not simply that he has comforted in the past, but he *comforts*.

The comfort we receive from God we may later use to comfort others. John Wesley wisely prayed, 'Let me not live to be useless.' What God permits to happen to us may be an answer to such a prayer and desire. Sometimes we may help others only as we ourselves have trodden the path they have to tread. For example, often we may effectively sympathise with the bereaved only when we have known bereavement ourselves. The comfort we seek to give to others that we have received from God in our personal times of trouble has a uniquely genuine ring. God knows from the beginning the people he is going to send across our path throughout our life. Nothing is ever wasted in God's school of suffering.

Paul lifts our sufferings to the highest level by referring to our sharing the sufferings of Christ (v. 5). We can never share in the redemptive sufferings of our Lord Jesus Christ, since they are utterly unique. He alone could die in our place. However, in the bringing of individuals to faith in him, and in their spiritual care and nurturing, the Lord Jesus uses his disciples. We cannot fulfil these privileged functions without costly distress of different kinds (*e.g.* 'the daily pressure . . . of . . . concern for all the churches' that Paul experienced – *2 Cor.* 11:28).

All involved in pastoral care of others soon discover how demanding such responsibility is. The sufferings of the Lord Jesus in this respect may flow over into our lives (v. 5), but this never happens without our comfort also overflowing! We may never be more aware of our Saviour's presence and help than when for his sake we engage in costly service of others.

Paul's philosophy emerges helpfully here (vv. 6–7). Paul was eager to share all this with the Corinthians. Some were no doubt anxious about the news of what had happened to him and his colleagues in their missionary endeavours. Paul freely admitted that they had known great distress. At the same time, he rejoiced because he was certain that the Corinthians and others would ultimately benefit. They would share the spiritual fruits of that distress. The experience of Paul and his friends would encourage the Corinthians to endure similar sufferings patiently as they witnessed the triumph of God's comfort.

PURPOSE NUMBER TWO:
God allows us to come to an end of ourselves, so that we may not rely on ourselves but on him – the God who raises the dead (vv. 8–9).

Part of Paul's purpose in writing to the Corinthians, with whom he had such a close relationship, was to keep in touch. They were among those who prayed for him and his fellow workers and who supported them in their work. Their labours in the province of Asia produced many hardships and sufferings. Paul's description implies considerable distress (vv. 8b–9). Some pressures of life and service seem beyond human ability to cope with; they threaten to crush or defeat us utterly.

Paul discerned God's purpose. He and his companions came to a complete end of themselves. In their hearts they 'felt . . . the sentence of death' (v. 9). In other words, they felt that there was no hope for them. They were at the end of their tether. It may have been so on the spiritual level. On the other hand, it may have been on the physical level that they were in desperate straits. Perhaps they experienced the complete collapse of health and felt their end was near. However, what Paul has already testified to in the previous verses proved true!

[8]

The experience was a waste neither for Paul and his partners nor for those who knew them. God gave them the necessary strength to endure. God allowed it all to happen so that they might not rely on themselves but on God, who raises the dead.

Self-confidence is a constant peril and danger. That is not to say that we should have no confidence in God-given abilities, strengths and gifts, or the experience of the past upon which we may call. But that confidence should never be to the point that we feel we can act independently of God or without looking to him to be our true strength and object of our praise. Self-reliance is perilous, and can be our downfall. God sometimes has to teach us through hard experiences not to rely on ourselves but on him. Having learnt the lesson, we may sometimes need to relearn it.

A fundamental principle emerges here. Basic to Christian faith and life is the resurrection of our Lord Jesus Christ. That is a truth to celebrate not only on Easter Day, but every day. If we put ourselves in the shoes of the first disciples after the crucifixion and before the resurrection, we can see the problem that the death of the Lord Jesus and his body resting in the grave presented to their hopes and aspirations. No problems, troubles, sufferings or perils we face are greater than those confronting those disciples. Yet God raised Jesus! That God is our God and Father! That Lord Jesus Christ is our risen and ascended Lord!

We must learn to put the truth of the resurrection up against, or alongside, every trouble and difficulty we face. In doing so, we fix our eyes upon God – and that is the first step to finding the answer we need in comfort, strength, endurance and victory! In many glorious senses we are the 'sons of the resurrection' (*Luke* 20:36)!

PURPOSE NUMBER THREE:
God teaches us to trust him as our deliverer, so that praise is brought to him (vv. 10–11).

Looking back on all the difficult experiences he has catalogued and hinted at, Paul bears testimony to God's deliverance (v. 10). 'He delivered us . . . and he will deliver us'. Paul deliberately set his hope on God's deliverance. To 'set one's hope' suggests disciplined determination and single-mindedness. It implies critical choice. Paul knew that the help he and his friends needed could come only from God, and to him alone therefore they looked. At the same time Paul knew that God gives a strategic place to the intercessory prayers of his people for deliverance.

Part of Christian fellowship is praying for one another. This is often more important than we appreciate. When our friends are going through times of trouble, they may find it hard to pray or to know for what to pray. God the Holy Spirit frequently – if not always – places upon the hearts of others the requests to be made to God for them. Those for whom we pray experience God's gracious favour – his blessing (v. 11) – as we intercede for them. Intercessory prayer is fundamental to the corporate life of God's people. Our prayers are part of God's rescue plan in his scheme of deliverance.

Answered prayers prompt thanksgiving to God (v. 11), and thanksgiving honours and glorifies him (*Psa.* 50:23). Looking back, Paul saw how the deliverance God afforded him and his companions through answered prayer brought praise to God. In this he glimpsed another of God's purposes in our troubles and sufferings: he uses them to bring praise to his name. God can have no higher end than his own praise. We can have no greater goal than God's glory.

PRAISE AND THANKSGIVING ARE GOD'S PROPER DUE

We may see now why Paul begins his letter with praise to God (v. 3). We must not minimise the reality of the afflictions (vv. 4,8), sufferings (vv. 5–7), burdens (v. 8) and perils (v. 10) that came to Paul and his friends and that also come to us. Nevertheless, we may learn to praise God in them all because of the good fruit they may produce.

Our difficulties are God-given opportunities to prove his compassion (v. 3), comfort (vv. 3–5, 7), power (v. 9), deliverance (v. 10), blessing (v. 11) and willingness to hear the prayers of his people (v. 11). How incredibly poor our experience of God's character as our glorious Father would be if we did not know trouble! How insubstantial would be the testimony we would be able to give to him! How little would be the praise and glory we would daily ascribe to him!

3

Paul's Change of Plans – A Matter of Integrity?

¹²For our boast is this, the testimony of our conscience, that we behaved in the world with simplicity and godly sincerity, not by earthly wisdom but by the grace of God, and supremely so toward you. ¹³For we are not writing to you anything other than what you read and acknowledge and I hope you will fully acknowledge— ¹⁴just as you did partially acknowledge us—that on the day of our Lord Jesus you will boast of us as we will boast of you.

¹⁵Because I was sure of this, I wanted to come to you first, so that you might have a second experience of grace. ¹⁶I wanted to visit you on my way to Macedonia, and to come back to you from Macedonia and have you send me on my way to Judea. ¹⁷Was I vacillating when I wanted to do this? Do I make my plans according to the flesh, ready to say 'Yes, yes' and 'No, no' at the same time? ¹⁸As surely as God is faithful, our word to you has not been Yes and No. ¹⁹For the Son of God, Jesus Christ, whom we proclaimed among you, Silvanus and Timothy and I, was not Yes and No, but in him it is always Yes. ²⁰For all the promises of God find their Yes in him. That is why it is through him that we utter our Amen to God for his glory. ²¹And it is God who establishes us with you in Christ, and has anointed us, ²²and who has also put his seal on us and given us his Spirit in our hearts as a guarantee.

²³But I call God to witness against me—it was to spare you that I refrained from coming again to Corinth. ²⁴Not that we lord it over your faith, but we work with you for your joy, for you stand firm in your faith.

¹For I made up my mind not to make another painful visit

to you. ²For if I cause you pain, who is there to make me glad but the one whom I have pained? ³And I wrote as I did, so that when I came I might not suffer pain from those who should have made me rejoice, for I felt sure of all of you, that my joy would be the joy of you all. ⁴For I wrote to you out of much affliction and anguish of heart and with many tears, not to cause you pain but to let you know the abundant love that I have for you (2 Cor. 1:12–2:4).

Paul's special relationship with the Corinthians was one he treasured. That was understandable because he witnessed the birth of the church in Corinth when, together with Silas and Timothy, he preached the gospel there. It was in Corinth that the Lord Jesus spoke to Paul in a memorable vision (*Acts* 18:9–11). 'The church of God that is at Corinth' (*2 Cor.* 1:1) was the consequence.

Relationships with our fellow believers bring unique joy; but if spoiled, they may also bring great sorrow. Those who ought to make us rejoice may sometimes distress us (*2 Cor.* 2:2–3). That was Paul's sad experience with the Corinthians. Out of his desire to keep in touch, Paul made promises to visit them (v. 16). The carrying out of Paul's intended plans to visit the Corinthians (see *1 Cor.* 16:5–9), however, had not been as straightforward as he had anticipated. Circumstances arose that meant he had not kept his promise. As a consequence, some of the Corinthians accused him of making his plans lightly, of promising to visit them without that purpose really being in his heart (v. 17).

In responding to the Corinthians' anxiety and false accusation, Paul indicates four constraints upon his character and behaviour that made him concerned for integrity in relationships.

CONSTRAINT NUMBER ONE

Paul knew he could not separate the reputation he had as a Christian from the good name and character of the God whom he represented and to whom one day he must answer. For the right reasons, Paul wanted the Corinthians to be able to boast of him and his colleagues, even as he and Silas and Timothy in turn could boast of God's work of grace in the Corinthians 'on the day of our Lord Jesus' (v. 14). The Corinthians knew enough of Paul's character from his stay with them to be able to boast of God's call of him to apostleship. The signs of apostleship – 'signs and wonders and mighty works' – were evident in his eighteen months in Corinth (*2 Cor.* 12:12). He likewise knew enough of the Corinthians to boast of God's grace at work in them because he witnessed the transformation of their lives through the gospel (cf. *1 Cor.* 6:9–11).

As we get to know and appreciate the genuineness of one another's holiness and sincerity, we are similarly able to boast of each other as the true work of God. The boasting is not in ourselves but in God. We know that the praise is not ours, but his. Paul needed to behave, as we all do, with the day of judgment in view. Although we may not always understand one another well now, 'on the day of our Lord Jesus' (v. 14) we shall know the truth about each other and our reputations. The final assessment of all character and conduct will be on that day.

CONSTRAINT NUMBER TWO

Paul knew that God – the God and Father of our Lord Jesus Christ, who has so wonderfully revealed himself to us in his Son – *is holy, sincere and faithful.* Paul uses the latter three adjectives of God in this passage (vv. 12, 18). God is holy (v. 12, margin), another name for his moral perfection. God's holiness precludes the possibility of him ever deceiving us. He is perfectly sincere in all his dealings with us.

The Greek word for 'sincere' comes from two words meaning 'warmth or light of the sun' and the verb 'to test', so that it literally means 'tested by sunlight', that is to say, pure. Looking at the windows in our home on a dull day, we may feel they are clean. When the sun shines, however, we see the truth – they are dirty! God is utterly flawless. He does not lie (*Titus* 1:2). He is completely faithful (v. 18), so that we may totally rely upon him. God's spiritual children, therefore, should reflect his holiness, sincerity and faithfulness in their character and conduct (vv. 12, 18).

With these thoughts in mind, Paul reminds the Corinthians of how he, Silas and Timothy preached the Lord Jesus when they were with them (v. 19). Having spent more than eighteen months in Corinth, the Corinthians had more opportunity than many other believers of hearing Paul's message and witnessing the kind of life he lived.

In preaching the Lord Jesus, Paul and his colleagues proclaimed the promises God makes in him (v. 20) – promises the Old Testament records, and promises the Lord Jesus himself gave during his ministry. They shared the lovely promises God makes to all believers about the Holy Spirit. God promises that his anointing of every believer with the Spirit is the seal of his ownership (vv. 21b–22). He promises that the indwelling of the Spirit is the guarantee of future glory (v. 22).

The use of seals goes back to the earliest of times. Owners branded both animals and people (like slaves) as a mark of ownership. Soldiers today wear badges to indicate the regiment to which they belong. The gift of the Holy Spirit to live in believers' hearts is a sign of God's complete ownership of them. It is also the pledge of the inheritance and salvation that belongs to them (cf. *Eph.* 1:13, 14; 4:30).

In proclaiming these promises in the Lord Jesus, Paul and his colleagues did not preach him as an uncertain Saviour who sometimes saves and other times does not. They did not suggest that occasionally God keeps his promises in him and other times goes back on them. All God's promises find their certain 'Yes' in Jesus. When we present our requests to God in view of his promises in the Lord Jesus, the answer is always 'Yes'. To every promise of God we, as believers, may add the name of Jesus and know that we have God's 'Yes' to it.

It is not surprising, therefore, that when we pray, we offer our prayers in the name of our Saviour and that our final word is 'Amen' – a word that simply and powerfully expresses the certainty and reliability of everything God promises us in his Son. We say our 'Amen' 'to God for his glory' (v. 20) because the praise and honour belong to God alone, since he gave his Son as the foundation of his great plan of salvation (*Rom.* 11:36).

How does what Paul says about God's character and promises relate to Paul's integrity? Such assurance about God's promises in Jesus had practical consequences for Paul's conduct – he had to strive to be as reliable in keeping his promises as God is to his. If Paul failed to be reliable, people might doubt the reliability of the God and Saviour he lived to proclaim.

CONSTRAINT NUMBER THREE

Paul was keenly aware of the important activity of his conscience (v. 12). Conscience has a habit of remembering things, and of reminding us of them at crucial moments. It is God's monitor in our soul. The Holy Spirit constantly educates our consciences by the Scriptures. He uses both the Bible and our conscience to convict us when our actions are wrong or inappropriate, as well as to confirm when they are right. Our conscience speaks about our conduct, our relationships to others, and our holiness, sincerity and faithfulness. Conscience is never to be ignored. The more we want to please God, the more we appreciate the good friend it is and the more we treasure God's Word.

CONSTRAINT NUMBER FOUR

Paul recognised that God's grace rather than earthly wisdom was to dictate his actions (v. 12). Daily life involves constantly making choices and promises. When we live by earthly, worldly wisdom we are inclined to ask, 'What is best for *me*? How may *I* profit from this situation?' When, however, we live in response to God's grace, we ask rather, 'What is in the best interests of God's people? What will most honour God, to whom I owe everything through Jesus Christ?'

If we live according to worldly wisdom, and perhaps have made mistakes, we may be inclined to massage the truth to avoid blame. Worldly wisdom is skilful at stating half-truths so that censure may be escaped. Spin doctors, individuals skilled in public relations, advise politicians and leaders on how to present their policies so that unfavourable aspects are hidden. God's grace, however, causes us to be truthful, to say what we mean, and to mean what we say. That is why Paul writes, 'we are not writing to you anything other than what you read and acknowledge' (v. 13). There was no double meaning in what he wrote to them.

THESE FOUR RESTRAINTS PROVIDE INSIGHT AS TO WHAT IT MEANS TO LIVE WITH INTEGRITY

First, we need to live with the day of judgment in view – 'the day of our Lord Jesus' (v. 14). It is wise to live every day as if the day of

[15]

judgment were tomorrow. *Second, we should conduct our relationships with the holiness, sincerity and faithfulness that are from God* (v. 12, 18). God the Holy Spirit wants to produce them in us as part of his essential fruit. *Third, we should acknowledge and obey our conscience as it speaks to us* (v. 12). It should always be viewed as a friend, never as an enemy. *Fourth, we should live not according to 'earthly wisdom but by the grace of God'* (v. 12).

These principles are relevant to all personal relationships. In marriage, for instance, we make promises, and we do it publicly in a wedding service. Whatever form of words we use, we promise to be a loving, faithful, and dutiful spouse 'for better, for worse; for richer, for poorer; in sickness and in health; to love and to cherish, until God separates us by death'. When a pastor is called to a church fellowship, usually in a public service of induction, pastor and people make promises of faithfulness to each other. When we come into church membership, we make a commitment to one another, in particular to love one another and to live in harmony no matter what the challenges may be. Integrity demands that we remain true to what we promise.

WHEN OUR RELATIONSHIPS GO WRONG OR OUR ACTIONS ARE MISUNDERSTOOD, WHAT SHOULD WE DO?

First, we must aim at honesty. What Paul has written about the Corinthians' misunderstanding of the postponement of his visit showed his desire to be honest and straightforward. That does not always come easily to us because it may not have been our habit.

Second, where possible, we must explain our actions and motives if we are in danger of being misunderstood. The desire to give such an explanation is itself an expression of the honesty at which we are to aim. Our explanation should be marked by simplicity, and not by the manipulative skills of worldly wisdom (vv. 12–14). There is no place for Christian spin doctors.

Part of Paul's honesty was to state the real reason he had not visited them again – it was to spare them pain (v. 23). If God-dishonouring behaviour in the church at Corinth had not been put right by the time of his visit, it was inevitable that he would have had to initiate disciplinary action. Paul's primary concern was the best interests of the Corinthians' faith. He wanted them to be strong in faith and in the obedience to God that true faith produces. A pastoral objective is to see believers persevere in the faith, to stand firm in the faith with joy (v. 24).

Paul made up his mind therefore that he would not make another painful visit to the Corinthians (*2 Cor.* 2:1). He wrote his earlier letter so that when he came he hopefully would not be distressed by those who ought to have made him rejoice (2:3). Letters often helpfully prepare the way for a visit. But misunderstood, they may misfire. Paul wrote his letter 'out of much affliction and anguish of heart and with many tears', not to grieve them but to let them know the depth of his love (2:4). Tears are a natural consequence of deep love. Nevertheless, his actions and motives were misunderstood. He was regarded as fickle in his promises. The questions were asked, 'Can Paul be trusted? Does he really care about us?' We may well wonder why and how such situations ever arise among God's people. Part of the answer is the unceasing activity of our spiritual enemy, Satan, described in the Book of Revelation as 'the accuser of our brothers' (*Rev.* 12:10).

The great lesson that arises from this passage is that our aim in our conduct – towards one another and towards the unbelieving world – is to reflect God's character. Although we know it is not fully attainable, we are to follow our Saviour's direction, 'You therefore must be perfect, as your heavenly Father is perfect' (*Matt.* 5:48). God is perfect in holiness, sincerity, and faithfulness (vv. 12, 18). We cannot all be gifted and outstandingly able. By the grace of God, however, we may all be men and women of integrity. God's promises in Jesus assure us of that!

4

Church Discipline and the Forgiveness of the Sinner

⁵Now if anyone has caused pain, he has caused it not to me, but in some measure—not to put it too severely—to all of you. ⁶For such a one, this punishment by the majority is enough, ⁷so you should rather turn to forgive and comfort him, or he may be overwhelmed by excessive sorrow. ⁸So I beg you to reaffirm your love for him. ⁹For this is why I wrote, that I might test you and know whether you are obedient in everything. ¹⁰Anyone whom you forgive, I also forgive. Indeed, what I have forgiven, if I have forgiven anything, has been for your sake in the presence of Christ, ¹¹so that we would not be outwitted by Satan; for we are not ignorant of his designs (2 Cor. 2:5–11).

One of the most difficult aspects of church life is the carrying out of spiritual discipline. The world regards it as an intrusion upon individual freedom. 'What right have you to judge others?' is the response of most non-Christians. Even Christians may be so unaccustomed to biblical teaching on its necessity that they also question its validity.

The Bible leaves us in no doubt about its importance. The church's responsibility is not to judge those outside the church, but those inside. Paul wrote about this in his first letter to the Corinthians (chapter 5). Sexual immorality was reported to have taken place among them, of a kind that did not occur even among pagans. A man had entered into a sexual relationship with his father's wife, that is to say, his stepmother. Paul expressed concern that the Corinthians had not been sufficiently grieved about the situation.

They failed to discipline the offending church member by putting him out of their fellowship. Paul instructed them to assemble as a church in the name of the Lord Jesus to administer appropriate discipline. The purpose of it was remedial – 'for the destruction of the flesh' so that the individual's 'spirit may be saved in the day of the Lord' (*1 Cor.* 5:5).

Church discipline takes seriously the pervasive power of wrong influence in the church (*1 Cor.* 5:6,7). Although the early example in 1 Corinthians 5 concerned sexual immorality, that is not the only ground for church discipline, although, sadly, it may be the most frequent. Grasping attitudes, idolatry, slander, drunkenness and swindling all constitute grounds for church discipline. Disputes between believers, false teaching and apostasy are further reasons for its exercise. Church discipline aims to promote the health of the whole church.

After giving his advice in his first letter, Paul became aware that the Corinthians had probably been too severe in discipline. We are uncertain of the individual's identity in this chapter. It may have been the person mentioned in 1 Corinthians 5. That has been the traditional view, although sometimes challenged.

On the other hand the person may have been someone who had made Paul the target of personal insults and about whom Paul had written in the letter that has been lost to us (v. 9). The first clue to this possibility is Paul's comment, 'Now if anyone has caused pain, he has caused it not to me, but in some measure—not to put it too severely—to all of you.' (v. 5). We get the impression that some of the Corinthians had been upset that the apostle, who had first preached the gospel to them, had – in his absence – been verbally abused. They may have felt more hurt than Paul ever did. 'Not to put it too severely' (v. 5b) seems to have the meaning, 'in order not to heap up too great a burden of words', that is to say, not to say too much. Perhaps the Corinthians had got something relatively minor out of proportion. If so, that seems to be more relevant to a personal insult than to the situation described in 1 Corinthians 5.

Another clue to the possibility of insult is the mention of Paul's personal grief (v. 10) and his words 'if I have forgiven anything'. Since presumably he had not heard the individual concerned make the insults and could respond only to hearsay, he was not convinced there was anything he had to forgive. Furthermore, he had corresponded with the Corinthians about the matter, giving directions about the proper reaction to such a situation. He had written to see if they would respond to his instructions about the exercise of church discipline. Their response was a good test of how obedient they were to Paul as an apostle (v. 9). Paul was not lording it over the Corinthians in requiring their obedience. That kind of authority was not given to him. Rather he had provided them with principles to apply to a difficult situation in Corinth. The obedience he looked for was obedience to God because the principles were right, and he had supplied them as the Lord Jesus Christ's representative.

Church discipline is an essential aspect of pastoral care. It begins with applications for church membership and is an important ground for establishing a church membership, rather than a casual relationship of belonging together.

When I applied to the elders for church membership, one of the questions I had to answer in the application form was, 'As a Christian, do you see the necessity of paying close attention to how you live (*Eph.* 5:15, *Rom.* 12:17), so as to lead a self-controlled and godly life (*Titus* 2:12), and to be an example of a Christian believer in your speech, conduct, love, faith, purity (*1 Tim.* 4:12) and separation from all that is dishonouring to God (*1 Cor.* 6:15–17)?' No Christian who wants to please God quarrels about the appropriateness of such questions. Every family requires discipline of some kind and needs to recognise which members of the family are to administer it. In the natural family it is usually the father and the mother. In the church family it is the pastor and elders. Every church family, like every human family, is made up of strong and weak members. Some may be weak because of inherent vulnerabilities, others because they are young in the faith, perhaps only recently converted from a lifestyle governed by the world's standards.

When we remember what we know about the city of Corinth, and the evil practices from which the Corinthians had been delivered (*1 Cor.* 6:9–11), it is not surprising that church discipline was necessary. Sins prevalent in the world inevitably threaten the life of the church, since its members have to live out their lives in its environment.

SEVEN PRINCIPLES

We may deduce a number of principles from this passage about church discipline. *First, the exercise of church discipline must be in the context of grief – corporate grief – about sin* (v. 5) *but with our feelings under control.* Paul acknowledges that hurt had been caused by the sin committed. That was entirely appropriate. What grieves God should grieve us. When the Spirit of God is pained by what happens, so should we be. Grief is a better response than anger. Anger is understandable, but it can distort our judgment. It is easy to be angry with the person who has sinned. The anger may be prompted as much by the trouble it causes us as the dishonour it brings to God's name. Grief is a better reaction than anger, but even then it must be controlled.

That is probably what Paul implies when he writes 'not to put it too severely' (v. 5). He was aware that we can get things out of perspective and say too much, or be too violent in our reactions. For this reason it is good to 'sleep on a situation' and not to act immediately, but rather to let our feelings, and the corporate reaction of a church fellowship, have time to settle. We frequently feel that something must be done at once. That is probably true, but 'at once' does not mean the actual moment we discover that something is wrong. The next day things are often not quite so desperate as they appeared at first. Furthermore, there is always a right way forward if honestly sought.

Second, church discipline demands a majority judgment and decision (v. 6). We do not know what is behind Paul's comment that the punishment inflicted on the individual 'by the majority is enough' (v. 6). Presumably it means that the church leadership at Corinth – *i.e.* the elders – brought the sin of this believer before the church, according to the pattern laid down in 1 Corinthians 5 and by our Lord Jesus Christ in Matthew 18:15–17. Then, whatever their procedure, disciplinary action was proposed and voted upon in some way. The majority concurred, and the decision was implemented.

Paul's words suggest that the decision was not unanimous. That may often be the case. Unanimity is a great blessing, but we must not demand it to the point that we do nothing whatsoever without it. We can never be sure, for example, that every Christian at a church meeting is walking with God and is in touch with him.

Personal factors may hinder Christians agreeing with the majority, especially friends or family of the offending member (for example, Eli's mistake, *1 Sam.* 2:22–25). Nevertheless, the decision of the majority is to be followed, since God gives his people corporate wisdom as they look to him. The mention of 'the majority', however, implies that a church must be in substantial agreement about the necessary action. At the same time, lack of complete unanimity must not preclude church discipline.

Third, church discipline requires applying an appropriate punishment (v. 6). The offending member at Corinth had been punished. He may have been put out of fellowship (see *1 Cor.* 5:2), or perhaps the privileges of church membership, such as sharing in the Lord's Supper, had been withdrawn from him until he proved his repentance. If he held any office or responsibility in the church, that privilege would have been removed from him. The task of those exercising church discipline is to determine the most appropriate punishment.

Fourth, the exercise of church discipline must have in view repentance and restoration, so that forgiveness and comfort may ultimately be given to the offending believer (v. 7). Paul was concerned that the punishment, or the spirit in which it was given, had been too severe. If so, the offender might have been 'overwhelmed by excessive sorrow' (v. 7). 'Overwhelmed' is the word used of Satan devouring people as a lion (*1 Pet.* 5:8), or of the waters of the Red Sea causing the Egyptians to be drowned (*Heb.* 11:29). Here it is used of a person's mental or spiritual state, since the individual may be filled with the despair of hopeless repentance. Satan delights to make a person under discipline feel that neither God nor his people love him and that there is no place for repentance and forgiveness (cf. *2 Cor.* 7:9).

Sorrow is a right response to our sin and part of our repentance concerning it. Overwhelming sorrow, however, that means we despair of being forgiven, and of ever putting things right, is not what God wants or what we should desire. Church discipline must be tempered with mercy. With the punishment the hope must be held out of repentance and restoration to fellowship.

There are two obvious dangers in church discipline: it may be too little or too much. If it is too little, it may not achieve the intended purpose. If it is too much, it may lead the offender to total despair.

Fifth, church discipline must have before it the hope of exercising Christian forgiveness – a forgiveness practised by all its members (v. 10). It would appear that the Corinthians may have maintained their punishment for too long. In view of the person's repentance, now was the time to forgive and comfort him (v. 7). They needed to reaffirm their love to him (v. 8), the love that God puts in our hearts for one another as members of his family. When discipline is properly exercised and accepted in the right spirit, the reaffirming of love is imperative. When a church fellowship recognises that discipline has done its work, and then exercises forgiveness, the task of every member is to be a part of that forgiveness. Paul assures the Corinthians that he identifies with them in their forgiveness. What others have forgiven, we must forgive.

Sixth, in exercising church discipline, we are to forgive as we have been forgiven, and as 'in the presence of Christ' (v. 10). This is another way of saying that it is to be done in a way that honours the Lord Jesus and reflects the manner in which he has already graciously forgiven us. It is to be done with the recognition that he is always present with his church by his Spirit. He walks among his candlesticks, the local churches (*Rev.* 2:1). Paul wanted to live his whole life 'in the presence of Christ', for this is at the heart of godliness for the individual as for the church. We are to forgive from our hearts, and to forgive as he has forgiven us. We may not be able to forget, but we must try to, and act as if we have.

Seventh, church discipline must be exercised with care, so that we do not give Satan an opportunity to outwit us (v. 11). We are not to be 'ignorant of his designs' (v. 11). He is always trying to outsmart us by his evil stratagems and tricks (cf. *Eph.* 6:11, *1 Pet.* 5:8). This is a timely warning and caution. If church discipline is insufficient, Satan is delighted because sin is then minimised and perhaps even encouraged. If church discipline is too severe, however, it may lead the offending individual to desperation and perhaps apostasy.

Satan so often strikes and gains entry into a church fellowship when we strive to do the right thing – as in church discipline – but go about it in the wrong way. If he can discourage us from doing our duty, he will. However, if he fails here, he will encourage us to go too far in doing our duty. He endeavours to turn something good into something bad. He delights in causing us to go to excess. He wants what we may know should be the proper cure (church discipline) to be worse in its consequences than the disease we try to remedy (the sin committed). We are not to be ignorant of how he works.

5

The Letters God Writes

[12] When I came to Troas to preach the gospel of Christ, even though a door was opened for me in the Lord, [13] my spirit was not at rest because I did not find my brother Titus there. So I took leave of them and went on to Macedonia.

[14] But thanks be to God, who in Christ always leads us in triumphal procession, and through us spreads the fragrance of the knowledge of him everywhere. [15] For we are the aroma of Christ to God among those who are being saved and among those who are perishing, [16] to one a fragrance from death to death, to the other a fragrance from life to life. Who is sufficient for these things? [17] For we are not, like so many, peddlers of God's word, but as men of sincerity, as commissioned by God, in the sight of God we speak in Christ.

[1] Are we beginning to commend ourselves again? Or do we need, as some do, letters of recommendation to you, or from you? [2] You yourselves are our letter of recommendation, written on our hearts, to be known and read by all. [3] And you show that you are a letter from Christ delivered by us, written not with ink but with the Spirit of the living God, not on tablets of stone but on tablets of human hearts.

[4] Such is the confidence that we have through Christ toward God. [5] Not that we are sufficient in ourselves to claim anything as coming from us, but our sufficiency is from God, [6] who has made us competent to be ministers of a new covenant, not of the letter but of the Spirit. For the letter kills, but the Spirit gives life (2 Cor. 2:12–3:6).

A sense of personal identity goes hand in hand with a sense of purpose in life. As we understand who we are, we are better able to understand how we should live. This passage shows how we are to view ourselves now that we have been born into God's family and are qualified to share in his Son's kingdom.

First and foremost, we are ministers or servants and proclaimers of a new covenant (3:6). The word used here for 'minister' or 'servant' describes someone who executes the commands of another. It is an appropriate word because it reminds us that the gospel – the good news of the new covenant – finds its origin not with us but with God.

A covenant is a binding agreement or contract. The Bible uses the word particularly of those obligations that God imposes upon himself, for the reconciliation of sinful men and women to him (*Gen.* 17:7, *Deut.* 7:6–9, *Heb.* 13:20). The covenant in both the Old and New Testaments is God's free decision to call out from the peoples of the world a people to be his own special possession, as he becomes their Redeemer.

When God made his covenants in the Old Testament, he committed himself to his people and called them to respond in obedience and loyalty. Sadly they failed to fulfil their reponsibility and so forfeited the blessings God had promised to those who were faithful to him. The new covenant, which was already announced in the Old Testament (*Jer.* 31:31–34), is both given to us by God and kept for us by Christ. At its heart is the atoning death of God's Son. At the Last Supper the Lord Jesus spoke of the cup of wine as representing the new covenant in his blood, poured out for his people (*Luke* 22:20). Under this covenant relationship, God declares, 'I will be their God, and they shall be my people' (*Heb.* 8:10). This covenant can never be broken, because it rests completely upon our Saviour's atoning sacrifice that sealed God's eternal covenant with all who believe in his Son. Paul unfolds the glory of this new covenant later, in the passage beginning at 3:7. Let us precede it with three statements that build upon each other.

1. The new covenant is ministered as the gospel of Christ is preached (2:12).

Gospel preaching was at the heart of all that Paul and his colleagues did. They knew it to be 'the gospel of Christ' (2:12). It is all about him, and the way in which God's grace is freely available to us through his Son's finished work upon the cross. The ministry of the new covenant is synonymous with the preaching of the gospel of Christ. The gospel proclaims that God has kept his promises, made in the Old Testament, of a new covenant open to men and women of every nation who turn to him in repentance and put their trust in the Messiah and Saviour, Jesus Christ our Lord.

For men and women to enter into this new covenant, however, the gospel has to be preached to them. Preaching, therefore, requires an emphasis upon 'going'. Our Saviour's words to his apostles were, 'All authority in heaven and on earth has been given to me. *Go* therefore and make disciples of all nations, baptizing them in the name of the Father and of the Son and of the Holy Spirit, teaching them to observe all that I have commanded you.' (*Matt.* 28:18–20; cf. *Mark* 16:15).

So it was that Paul 'came to Troas to preach the gospel of Christ' (2:12). Troas was a port near Troy in northwest Turkey, in northern Asia Minor. It was there that Paul had his dream of the man from Macedonia (*Acts* 16:8–10) and where he restored Eutychus to life (*Acts* 20:5–11). Paul's going to Troas was part of his obedience to his Master's commission. His ambition was 'to preach the gospel, not where Christ has already been named', so that he would not 'build on someone else's foundation' (*Rom.* 15:20).

As God's people are prepared to obey his Son's final commission to preach the gospel, so God prepares the way for them. When Paul arrived in Troas he found 'a door was opened . . . in the Lord' for him (2:12). By this he presumably meant that people welcomed him and were ready to listen. As in Philippi, the Lord opened people's hearts to receive the gospel. As we are messengers of the new covenant in obedience to God, we are to expect him to open doors of opportunity.

We must not forget that the background to the early part of this letter is Paul's explanation of why he had not yet kept his promise to visit the Corinthians again. He therefore felt bound to explain in some detail why he left Troas and travelled on to Macedonia. The explanation was that he had expected to find Titus in Troas, but he was disappointed (2:13). He regarded Titus with great affection – 'my brother' (2:13). Not finding Titus at Troas, Paul had no peace of mind to remain, and so he moved on to Macedonia, no doubt hoping to find Titus there. We may sometimes be distracted from seizing a God-given opportunity for the gospel because we lack peace of mind. No doubt Paul's feelings were influenced by his concern for Titus and the value of working together.

Nevertheless, Paul expresses at this point his thanks to God because he is in charge of our disappointments! William Cowper's hymn so wisely puts it, 'Behind a frowning providence he hides a smiling face.' Paul had sufficient experience of God's providence to know that God works out his purposes through our frustrations.

Besides being an expression of thanks, verse 14 is also a declaration of faith. 'But thanks be to God, who in Christ always leads us in triumphal procession, and through us spreads the fragrance of the knowledge of him everywhere.' More important than human disappointments as we obediently preach the gospel is its expansion. To proclaim the good news is to spread the knowledge of Christ (2:14). Again, we are reminded that the gospel is all about him. That knowledge has delightful and unique fragrance (2:14). Whatever happens to God's servants, God sees to it that through their experiences, including disappointments, the fragrance of his Son is spread everywhere.

Through such preaching God leads us 'in triumphal procession' in Christ (2:14). The Corinthians knew all about Roman 'triumphal processions' or 'triumphs'. These were parades given in honour of Roman generals who won outstanding victories over their enemies. They had perhaps gained new lands for Rome, as well as bringing home valuable spoils and booty. The successful general rode in a golden chariot accompanied by his soldiers and the captives they had taken. Our Lord Jesus won the victory over all his enemies by his cross and resurrection. As we, his servants, preach the gospel – that is to say, exercise the ministry of the new covenant – we proclaim his victory and gather to him the great company of people of every nation whom the Father has promised him.

The fragrance (2:14) and aroma (2:15) are all part of the picture. As a Roman triumph progressed, priests filled censers with burning incense. This meant life to the victorious soldiers because they were sharing in their leader's triumph, but it meant death to the captives heading for the arena. To those who receive the message of the gospel we are 'the fragrance of Christ', for we bring them the good news about him, 'the fragrance from life to life' (2:16). But to those who reject him and the good news about him, we bring the smell of death. To be without Christ is to be without hope in the world. To reject him is to be doomed to destruction.

When you are walking down a street, an especially attractive fragrance may make you turn your head to find where it is coming from. Our lives should bear such a fragrance of our Lord Jesus that people are compelled to look for the source. Significantly, this statement about being led always in triumph is set in the context of afflictions (1:8) and being 'utterly burdened' (1:8), to the point of feeling the sentence of death within oneself (1:9). A fragrance is sometimes only possible when a fruit or kernel is crushed.

Paul was in no doubt about the certainty of the success of gospel preaching and its eternal consequences. 'God . . . in Christ always leads us in triumphal procession' (2:14) as we proclaim the gospel. For some it will mean salvation, and for others death and eternal separation from God (2:16). Salvation is synonymous with eternal life (2:16). As the gospel is faithfully offered to people, and they refuse it, those who share the gospel with them become the smell of death instead of the fragrance of life (2:16). No wonder Paul exclaims, 'Who is sufficient for these things?' (2:16) To have the gospel committed to us for the world's benefit is an onerous responsibility.

Three aspects of the outworking of our responsibility are highlighted. *First, we are to speak as those who are 'in Christ'* (2:17). Nothing has more significance than our union with the Lord Jesus. This is part of the wonder of salvation. As we speak to others, we are to speak in the light of our union with him, and in dependence upon him. United with him, we share his triumph as we proclaim his gospel.

Our second responsibility is godly integrity – speaking 'as men of sincerity, as commissioned by God' (2:17). Godliness is doing what is right with an eye to God's approval alone. When we share the gospel, we are not to have an eye upon people's approval but God's. That is especially relevant when we explain the seriousness of sin and God's judgment upon it. If we have an eye upon human approval, we may be tempted to water down the solemn and awe-inspiring aspects of our subject; but not if we speak as in God's sight, with a view to pleasing him in what we say. Such determination will mean that personal motives of gain or advantage find no place in our sharing of the gospel.

Satan aims at corrupting our best endeavours. He encourages people, where he can, to peddle the word of God for profit (2:17). While the Lord Jesus established the principle that 'the labourer deserves his wages' (*Luke* 10:7, *1 Cor.* 9:14) that does not mean that his representatives should offer the Word of God for money. Those who strive to live as in God's sight do not do so. Paul made it plain that he did not covet anyone's money or possessions. To make that clear, he worked with his hands to pay his way and to supply the needs of his colleagues. He exemplified the words of the Lord Jesus that 'It is more blessed to give than to receive' (*Acts* 20:33–35; cf. *1 Thess.* 2:3–5). Covetousness can spoil the best things, as both history and experience show.

Third, when we share the gospel, we are to speak as those who are sent by God. The authority with which we speak is not our own, but God's. We are only messengers, but we must ensure that we convey the message accurately – what Paul described to the Ephesian elders as 'the whole counsel of God' (*Acts* 20:27).

2. As the new covenant is ministered – as the gospel is preached – fruit is produced in people's lives. Transformed lives then authenticate the message and the messengers (3:1–3).

Questions raised about Paul's apostleship are the background to this assertion. As indicated earlier, some at Corinth questioned the genuineness of his apostleship. His relationship with the Corinthians was at times fragile. They tended to forget their part of the special relationship that existed between them and the evidences they had witnessed of his apostleship.

While much of what Paul writes answers such questions, he recognised that self-commendation has no place in the Christian life. We should always be suspicious when people presume to commend themselves. It is out of character for a Christian, since it is contrary to the example of our Lord Jesus. If approval has any place, it is when it comes from others, not from ourselves (3:1; cf. *Rom.* 16:1).

The best commendation of servants of the gospel is the transformed lives of those who receive it through them. Their lives then become like letters (3:2). First, they are letters written on the hearts of the messengers themselves (3:2). Their conversion rejoices their hearts, and assures and renews their call to preach it. Second, the transformed lives of the recipients of the gospel constitute letters that all may scrutinise. What the gospel does for people is so remarkable that their lives become open letters in which to discover the power and grace of God.

If a letter of commendation for Paul and his colleagues was required, the Corinthians' transformed lives constituted it! They were letters written not with ink on paper, but letters written by the Holy Spirit on human hearts (3:3). It is there that the Holy Spirit works, and the change that comes in life and behaviour issues from changed hearts. The Holy Spirit writes his testimonies to God's power not on tablets of stone but on tablets of human hearts. The New Testament provides illuminating and telling illustrations of what the church is to be in the world, and this is one. The church is like a personal letter that our Lord Jesus Christ sends to the world proclaiming what he can do in human lives. True Christian witness is the witness of transformed men and women. Our lives are to be like open letters that anyone may read, in which we testify to our Saviour's power (3:2).

Attacks upon his apostleship prompted Paul to give this picture. Ordinary human letters of recommendation were not sufficient to assure people of his apostleship. He did not require such, and he did not need to stand up for himself. Christian ministry and service are not authenticated by human credentials but by their spiritual fruit. The Corinthian believers therefore constituted Paul and his colleagues' 'letter of recommendation' (3:2).

All who engage in the ministry of the new covenant receive God-given proof of their calling. We are to have this confidence through Christ before God (3:4). This is quite different from self-confidence. God himself makes us competent ministers of the new covenant, and this gives us confidence (3:5). As we recognise our own inadequacy, we are in a position to discover God as the source of our adequacy. He makes us competent 'not of the letter but of the Spirit. For the letter kills, but the Spirit gives life ' (3:6). The law – that is to say, 'the letter' – can only condemn us, but the new covenant in Christ gives life by the Spirit. The written law is not replaced but the Spirit gives power to fulfil it as God intends. The Holy Spirit's work is essential to the new covenant, and to our sharing of it in gospel preaching. Spiritual life – new birth – is the fruit of that covenant. It comes about as people receive the good news of the Lord Jesus. This new covenant generates not legalism, but liberty and life (3:6). Who would not want to share in this ministry? It is our great privilege and God's calling to us in his Son.

3. To exercise such a ministry, our Lord Jesus Christ himself must be central.

Everywhere we look in this passage, we witness the centrality of the Lord Jesus. He is the centre at which God's promises and our faith meet. The gospel is *his* (2:12). God leads us in triumphal procession *in Christ* (2:14). Through us, his people, God spreads everywhere *the fragrance of the knowledge of Christ* (2:14). We are *the aroma of Christ* in the world (2:15). It is *in Christ* that we speak before God with sincerity (2:17). The proper consequences of our ministry are letters *from Christ* (3:3), that is to say, transformed lives that proclaim messages and truths *about him*. Our confidence for this whole wonderful ministry is *through Christ* (3:4). We may recognise therefore why it is that 'there is nothing that Satan tries so hard to do as to raise up mists to obscure Christ; for he knows that by this means the way is opened up for every kind of falsehood' (John Calvin).

The old maxim remains true:

> 'What think ye of Christ?' is the test
> To try both your state and your scheme;
> You cannot be right in the rest
> Unless you think rightly of him.

6

The Glory of the New Covenant

7Now if the ministry of death, carved in letters on stone, came with such glory that the Israelites could not gaze at Moses' face because of its glory, which was being brought to an end, 8will not the ministry of the Spirit have even more glory? 9For if there was glory in the ministry of condemnation, the ministry of righteousness must far exceed it in glory. 10Indeed, in this case, what once had glory has come to have no glory at all, because of the glory that surpasses it. 11For if what was being brought to an end came with glory, much more will what is permanent have glory.

12Since we have such a hope, we are very bold, 13not like Moses, who would put a veil over his face so that the Israelites might not gaze at the outcome of what was being brought to an end. 14But their minds were hardened. For to this day, when they read the old covenant, that same veil remains unlifted, because only through Christ is it taken away. 15Yes, to this day whenever Moses is read a veil lies over their hearts. 16But when one turns to the Lord, the veil is removed. 17Now the Lord is the Spirit, and where the Spirit of the Lord is, there is freedom. 18And we all, with unveiled face, beholding the glory of the Lord, are being transformed into the same image from one degree of glory to another. For this comes from the Lord who is the Spirit (2 Cor. 3:7–18).

A school project may involve children asking grandparents and others what it was like to live as children during the Second World War. That is useful for the study of history, and it also helps those who have lived only in times of peace to appreciate a little of what it meant to live in a period of war. Living as we do after the coming of our Lord Jesus Christ into the world and the establishment of the new covenant, it is difficult for us to understand fully what it must have meant to live in the world before that great event – in the period of the old covenant. Paul draws comparisons now between the old and the new covenants to demonstrate the superior nature and glory of the new. Having established that God 'has made us competent to be ministers of a new covenant' (v. 6), he explains its glory. We often appreciate something better by means of contrast, particularly when we want to demonstrate how radically different it is. Paul draws four comparisons.

THE FIRST COMPARISON:
The old covenant brought death and condemnation, whereas the new brings life and righteousness (vv. 7–9).

Basic to the old covenant was God's giving of his law. That law is a perfect reflection of his righteous and holy character. As Isaiah explains, 'The Lord was pleased, for his righteousness' sake, to magnify his law and make it glorious' (*Isa.* 42:21). God did not give his law as an impossible obstacle to our obtaining righteousness and eternal life. Rather he gave it because it perfectly reveals and reflects his nature. Our duty is to obey it. The promise of eternal life was made to those who fulfil it. God said, 'keep my statutes and my rules; if a person does them, he shall live by them' (*Lev.* 18:5). History and personal experience demonstrate the impossibility of perfect obedience to God's law. As a consequence we merit God's punishment and condemnation – we deserve to die. 'The ministry' of the old covenant, therefore, was 'of death' (v. 7). 'Carved in letters on stone' and given with 'glory', as it was, it brought about the government or rule of death because we cannot keep it. The straight edge of the law shows how crooked we are (*Gal.* 3:24). The proof the law gives of our sinfulness proves crucial in our Christian experience, since the needle of the law makes way for the thread of the gospel.

The law, therefore, shows us our need of the gospel of the new covenant. All who strive to obey God's law as a means of gaining acceptance with him soon discover that it is not achievable. However, the wonder of the new covenant is that what our Lord

[34]

Jesus achieved by his saving work on the cross marks the end of the struggle for righteousness by law-keeping for everyone who believes in him (see, for example, *Rom.* 10:4). God himself, through his Son's atoning work, sets everything right between him and us by counting Christ's righteousness to us – the actual righteousness of his Son (v. 9; cf. *Phil.* 3:9). To use the familiar New Testament description of a Christian, we are 'in Christ'. The Lord Jesus achieved all that is necessary for our justification before God through the reckoning to us of his righteousness. As a consequence, we are delivered from the government of death and live instead in the realm of God's life-giving Spirit.

THE SECOND COMPARISON:
The old covenant had a fading glory, whereas that of the new lasts (vv. 10–11).

To understand and appreciate this second comparison, we must go to the Old Testament. The old covenant was given to Moses for the people when God gave him his law. It was accompanied 'with glory' (v. 7). Important events preceded and accompanied it. Exodus 24 begins 'Then he said to Moses, "Come up to the Lord, you and Aaron, Nadab, and Abihu, and seventy of the elders of Israel, and worship from afar. Moses alone shall come near to the Lord, but the others shall not come near, and the people shall not come up with him."' (*Exod.* 24:1–2). The old covenant revealed God's holiness in a righteous standard of law that those who receive it are solemnly ordered to keep.

The giving of the law was an essential part of the old covenant God established with Israel. At the heart of it was what we know as the Ten Commandments. The covenant specified in these ten major commandments – and in scores of lesser ones – the behaviour God required of Israel in the covenant relationship. It also declared both the curses that would come upon them if they broke its terms, and the blessings that would follow if they kept them. Moses carefully told the people *all* the Lord's words and laws (*Exod.* 24:3). He wrote down *everything* the Lord said (*Exod.* 24:4). The old covenant was established upon the assumption of the people's obedience, an obedience they promised (*Exod.* 24:3).

The importance of the covenant relationship was underlined in two ways. First, the covenant relationship needed to be written down. We have, therefore, *the Book of the Covenant* (*Exod.* 24:7) – the record of all God said and established in his covenant relationship.

Second, the covenant relationship required to be sealed or ratified – and so we have *the blood of the covenant* (*Exod.* 24:8). Immediately after writing down all the Lord had said, Moses 'built an altar at the foot of the mountain, and twelve pillars, according to the twelve tribes of Israel. And he sent young men of the people of Israel, who offered burnt offerings and sacrificed peace offerings of oxen to the Lord. And Moses took half of the blood and put it in basins, and half of the blood he threw against the altar. Then he took the Book of the Covenant and read it in the hearing of the people. And they said, "All that the Lord has spoken we will do, and we will be obedient." And Moses took the blood and threw it on the people and said, "Behold the blood of the covenant that the Lord has made with you in accordance with all these words."' (*Exod.* 24:4–8).

Blood ritual was common to most forms of covenant. The custom continues still in cultures where 'blood brothers' are made by allowing blood from two persons to mingle and flow together in one.

The book of Exodus gives no explanation of the blood ritual, and so we can only guess at its significance. It may be that God and the people were reckoned as of 'one blood' and that God declared himself to be their 'father' and 'redeemer'. Or the blood ritual may have been the equivalent of the people invoking death upon themselves if the terms of the covenant were not kept. But we do not know. So that the people would not forget what he had given them in his law and in the promises they made, God gave them his law in tablets of stone (*Exod.* 24:12–18), elsewhere called 'the tablets of the covenant' (*Deut.* 9:9).

The glory of God settled on Mount Sinai at the giving of the law, and it was symbolised by the cloud that covered it (*Exod.* 24:16). God's glory looked like a consuming fire on top of the mountain (*Exod.* 24:17). The old covenant was a two–party covenant. God had his part to play, with his conditions to fulfil, and the Israelites had theirs. It was plain from the start that if the Israelites broke their part of the covenant and failed to meet its demands, they would not only forfeit the blessings God promised, but they would ruin their relationship with him and bring down his curses upon their heads. Sadly, that is precisely what they did!

Something significant occurred as God established the old covenant. Moses' face shone with its reflection of God's glory (vv. 7–8). The glory mirrored in his face indicated the glory of the gift that God was giving them in his law and covenant. Moses received it on behalf of the people. The glory seen in Moses' face, however, faded, as did the glory of the law, since it served to condemn men and women because of their disobedience (v. 9). Nevertheless, the glory of the law is great. It was, and is, an immeasurable gift. Where would we be without it in our understanding of God and of the appropriate behaviour of his creatures?

We now come to the heart of this second comparison (vv. 9–11): 'For if there was glory in the ministry of condemnation, the ministry of righteousness must far exceed it in glory. Indeed, in this case, what once had glory has come to have no glory at all, because of the glory that surpasses it. For if what was being brought to an end came with glory, much more will what is permanent have glory.'

What was glorious in the old has no glory now in comparison with the surpassing glory of the new (v. 10). It is not that the old covenant had no glory, but in comparison with the new it would *seem* as if it had none! The glory of the new covenant is a *surpassing* glory (v. 10). The old covenant was a temporary arrangement, whereas the new is eternal (v. 11). The righteousness God reckons to us through faith in the Lord Jesus is for ever! The blood of the Lord Jesus by which we are saved is 'the blood of the *eternal* covenant' (*Heb.* 13:20).

The fading glory of the old covenant was expressed and illustrated, therefore, by the manner in which the reflected glory on Moses' face faded (v. 13). He put a veil over his face to keep the Israelites from gazing at it while the radiance was fading away. His action symbolised the fading glory of the old covenant (v. 13).

THE THIRD COMPARISON:
The old covenant brought despair, fear and bondage, whereas the new brings hope, boldness and freedom (vv. 12–15).

Countless men and women throughout the centuries have passionately sought to be right with God by striving after perfect obedience to his law. Theoretically this endeavour holds promise, but in practice it proves impossible. As a consequence, such efforts breed despair. The more we try, the more aware we become of failure. With failure and despair come fear and bondage. The fear is the fear of judgment. 'The soul who sins shall die' is the Old Testament declaration (*Ezek.* 18:4). After death comes judgment, and sinners have no hope of acceptance by God at the judgment if their confidence is in what they themselves have achieved.

We may be wondering, 'If the old covenant brought so much despair, fear and bondage, what about people like Abraham, David and all the heroes of the Old Testament recorded in Hebrews 11?' The answer is straightforward and profound. God did not begin to be the God of grace with the dawn of our Saviour's coming. Grace is an essential aspect of his eternal character. He had always been such, and at the moment of Adam and Eve's rebellion he made the gracious promise of a Saviour (*Gen.* 3:15).

In the centuries that followed, God made people aware of their need of forgiveness and its provision through atonement. He instituted the sacrificial system that pointed ultimately to the Lord Jesus as the Lamb of God. The first promises were built upon, and added to, until the wonder of God's plan was seen in prophecies like Isaiah 53. People such as Abraham and David believed God and his promises (*Rom.* 4:1–8) In repentance and faith they obediently offered the atoning sacrifices God laid down, some- times sensing that they were the shadows of a far greater reality. God graciously made them aware of their acceptance. God's promises to them were real, but better and greater were to come.

How different in comparison are the promises belonging to those under the new covenant! We have hope (v. 12), that is to say, confidence and assurance for the future. The glory of what we now possess in the Lord Jesus lasts (v. 11). As Paul expressed it elsewhere, 'We rejoice in hope of the glory of God' (*Rom.* 5:2). We shall see our Saviour's glory and share in it! 'Beloved, we are God's children now, and what we will be has not yet appeared; but we know that when he appears we shall be like him, because we shall see him as he is.' (*1 John* 3:2).

With such a glorious hope comes boldness (v. 12) – the boldness of God's children in prayer. We do not have to be uncertain about

God's acceptance of us; we may be assured of it. He does not receive us for our own sakes, but for his Son's. 'We have confidence to enter the holy places by the blood of Jesus, by the new and living way that he opened for us through the curtain, that is, through his flesh' (*Heb.* 10:20,21). The Holy Spirit encourages us with boldness to cry, '*Abba*, Father.' The Scriptures he has inspired encourage us: 'Let us then with confidence draw near to the throne of grace, that we may receive mercy and find grace to help in time of need.' (*Heb.* 4:16). Possessing reverent boldness before God, we have boldness in witness before men and women in the world (cf. *Acts* 4:31). As we are expectant in prayer before God we become fearless before the world.

THE FOURTH COMPARISON:
The old covenant did not even enable men and women to look at Moses' face when it reflected God's glory, whereas the new enables us to see the glory of Christ and to be transformed by it.

This glorious benefit of the new covenant is beyond words to express. Paul refers to what the Book of Exodus describes. Moses' face shone with the reflected glory of God when he received the law (*Exod.* 34:29–30, 33, 35). The Israelites, however, could not look steadily at his face, fading though its glory was (*2 Cor.* 3:7).

Before continuing his comparison, Paul pauses for a moment to refer to and explain the position of Jews who stand outside the new covenant. Every true Jew looks forward to the fulfilment of God's promises of a new covenant (*Jer.* 31:31–34) and the Messiah's coming to achieve it. Sadly, the majority in the first century and the centuries that followed have failed to see the fulfilment of those promises in the coming of the Lord Jesus.

Paul takes up the picture of the veil that covered Moses' face to illustrate the position of Jews who do not yet believe in the Lord Jesus as their Messiah and Saviour. Like the veil that Moses put over his face to keep the Israelites from gazing at it, a veil covers their hearts when the old covenant is read (v. 15) so that they do not appreciate the truth of their situation. They foolishly put their trust in their orthodoxy or obedience instead of trusting in God's

Son. While the veil is in place, their minds are dull (v. 14). The veil is taken away only when they turn to the Lord in conversion (v. 16). The Holy Spirit is the One who works in hearts to remove the veil (vv. 16–17). He is always involved when anyone turns to the Lord. In praying for Israel, we should pray that the veil will be taken away and that they will see (v. 16).

Now we must return to the comparison. When the veil is removed from our hearts by the Holy Spirit, he shows us the glory of the Lord Jesus. As Paul explains in the next chapter, God, who said 'Let light shine out of darkness,' shines 'in our hearts to give the light of the knowledge of the glory of God in the face of Jesus Christ' (*2 Cor.* 4:6). The Lord Jesus uniquely brings before the eyes of our heart the glory of God, and we are enthralled and captivated by it.

Under the old covenant, men and women could not even look at God's reflected glory in Moses' face. However, under the new we may look with perfect freedom upon the glory of God in our Saviour's face. God the Holy Spirit delights to turn our eyes to the Lord Jesus so that we consider him.

Looking is a way of becoming. As we contemplate the Lord Jesus, a glorious miracle takes place: we become like him in character. Our lives are intended to become brighter and more attractive as we become more and more like him (v. 18). Becoming like him, we reflect his glory. The glory of the new covenant is that our reflecting of the Lord's glory has the potential for always increasing, in marked contrast to the sadly fading glory of the old.

Familiar as we tend to be with the Bible in its two parts – the Old and New Testaments (*i.e.* covenants) – we probably overlook all too often the wonder of living under the New. One evening in an upper room, the Lord Jesus took wine and said, 'This cup that is poured out for you is the new covenant in my blood' (*Luke* 22:20). The promise of Jeremiah 31:31–34 saw its fulfilment at Calvary. At the Lord's Supper we are reminded of how important is our regular proclamation of this new covenant.

7

Why We Do Not Give Up

¹Therefore, having this ministry by the mercy of God, we do not lose heart. ²But we have renounced disgraceful, underhanded ways. We refuse to practice cunning or to tamper with God's word, but by the open statement of the truth we would commend ourselves to everyone's conscience in the sight of God. ³And even if our gospel is veiled, it is veiled only to those who are perishing. ⁴In their case the god of this world has blinded the minds of the unbelievers, to keep them from seeing the light of the gospel of the glory of Christ, who is the image of God. ⁵For what we proclaim is not ourselves, but Jesus Christ as Lord, with ourselves as your servants for Jesus' sake. ⁶For God, who said, 'Let light shine out of darkness,' has shone in our hearts to give the light of the knowledge of the glory of God in the face of Jesus Christ.

⁷But we have this treasure in jars of clay, to show that the surpassing power belongs to God and not to us. ⁸We are afflicted in every way, but not crushed; perplexed, but not driven to despair; ⁹persecuted, but not forsaken; struck down, but not destroyed; ¹⁰always carrying in the body the death of Jesus, so that the life of Jesus may also be manifested in our bodies. ¹¹For we who live are always being given over to death for Jesus' sake, so that the life of Jesus also may be manifested in our mortal flesh. ¹²So death is at work in us, but life in you.

¹³Since we have the same spirit of faith according to what has been written, 'I believed, and so I spoke,' we also believe, and so we also speak, ¹⁴knowing that he who raised the Lord Jesus will raise us also with Jesus and bring us with you into his presence. ¹⁵For it is all for your sake, so that as grace extends to more and more people it may increase thanksgiving, to the glory of God.

[16]So we do not lose heart. Though our outer self is wasting away, our inner self is being renewed day by day. [17]For this light momentary affliction is preparing for us an eternal weight of glory beyond all comparison, [18]as we look not to the things that are seen but to the things that are unseen. For the things that are seen are transient, but the things that are unseen are eternal (2 Cor. 4:1–18).

2 Corinthians is the most personal of Paul's letters: in it he reveals his feelings more than in any other. The letter shows that misunderstandings damaged his relationship to the Corinthians and grieved him greatly. Paul was greatly discouraged. Nevertheless, he did not give up! He explains why he and his companions persevered in spite of many obstacles.

'Therefore, having this ministry by the mercy of God, we do not lose heart' (v. 1). His theme remains the ministry of the gospel and Christian responsibility for evangelism throughout the world. The truth that held him steady no matter what the opposition or difficulties was that he and his colleagues had received this ministry 'by the mercy of God' (v. 1). Our experience of God's mercy in his Son is the source of our personal knowledge of God. In his letter to the Romans, it is 'by the mercies of God' that Paul appeals to us to offer our bodies to God as living sacrifices (*Rom.* 12:1). Here in 2 Corinthians it is the secret of his refusal to give up when difficulties arise.

Grace and mercy are closely related and sometimes almost interchangeable. They are, however, different. Grace pardons, while mercy empathises and consoles. Grace is God's love to the guilty; mercy is his love towards the distressed. It is because God in his mercy feels for us in our distress that he shows his grace in pardoning our sins and relieving us from our greatest danger. The Lord Jesus is the most wonderful gift of God's mercy to us, and every other gracious benefit flows from that immeasurable gift. There is more mercy in the Lord Jesus than there is sin in us. The more we contemplate God's mercy in his Son, the more committed we want to be to his service and the gospel.

Nevertheless, we meet with discouragements. Things happen in our service of God that upset and disturb us. For instance, when key workers in the church fellowship have to move away, we can be discouraged. Paul, however, had far greater grounds for discouragement in view.

COUNTERFEIT GOSPELS

First, counterfeit gospels exist. Paul implies this when he declares, 'But we have renounced disgraceful, underhanded ways. We refuse to practice cunning or to tamper with God's word' (v. 2). When we proclaim the gospel of our Lord Jesus, we are in conflict not only with ignorance but, worse still, with counterfeit gospels. Throughout the history of the church, the gospel has been counterfeited by false emphases and teachings. Counterfeiters engage in 'disgraceful, underhanded ways'. Teachings and practices, often dishonouring to God, take place out of public view.

It is natural to be upset by counterfeits, and it is fitting that we should be. Opponents of the gospel are often underhand in the way they go about things, deliberately manipulating people and acting shamefully. They may profess to obey God's Word while at the same time distorting the Scriptures and practising deception. It is a discouragement to meet people who profess to teach God's truth and the gospel of his Son, but who turn out to be deceivers. The world is sadly full of counterfeit 'gospels' or doctrines. Those who put forth bogus teaching tend to focus upon human personalities or to preach themselves (v. 5). However, we must not miss an important consolation: forgeries exist only because the reality they counterfeit is so valuable!

SPIRITUAL BATTLE

Second, we are engaged in a spiritual battle with the god of this world (vv. 3–4). Behind all counterfeit teachings and 'gospels' is the activity of the enemy of souls, Satan. He tries to obscure the true message of the gospel, to place 'a veil' over the minds of men and women so that they cannot see or understand the good news. He wants them to perish (v. 3). To this end, he blinds 'the minds of the unbelievers, to keep them from seeing the light of the gospel of the glory of Christ, who is the image of God.' (v. 4).

It is specifically the glory of the Lord Jesus, the image of God, that Satan does not want people to understand (v. 4). This explains the unique and unusual opposition we may often sense when we determine to proclaim the Lord Jesus to people. The evil one is not particularly concerned when we talk about religion, or even Christianity, but he is disturbed when we proclaim the Lord Jesus and his unique glory as 'the image of God'.

HUMAN WEAKNESS

Third, weakness and frailty characterise us (v. 7). Paul pictures our bodies as 'jars of clay', an image of fragility. We are ordinary people with ordinary people's vulnerabilities. It is amazing to think that God commits the stewardship of his Son's gospel to such commonplace people as ourselves! Our opponents may often appear better equipped to achieve their aims than we are ours. Not many of us are wise by human standards; not many of us are influential or important as the world reckons (*1 Cor.* 1:26–27).

HARD PRESSED

Fourth, we are afflicted in all kinds of ways (vv. 8–10). We are sometimes under pressure on every side, perplexed, persecuted, and struck down (vv. 8,9). What people did to our Lord Jesus they may do to us, so that every day we reveal and share in the death of our Saviour (v. 10). We put ourselves at risk for him, so that death may be said to be at work in us (v. 12). Not all of these experiences may be ours, but they are the lot of Christians elsewhere in the world.

WEAR AND TEAR

Fifth, because of all these potential discouragements, we know the wear and tear of the spiritual battle. It takes its toll upon us. 'Our outer nature is wasting away' (v. 16). Although the conflict is essentially spiritual, it takes its physical toll. Sometimes it may look as if everything is falling apart. We may catch glimpses of just how weak our bodies are and the strain our service imposes on them.

TROUBLES

Sixth, we have our troubles (v. 17). We would be dishonest if we did not admit their existence. We undergo the trauma all men and women experience in a fallen world. We are as vulnerable to disease and accident as others. Additional troubles arise from our Christian faith and testimony. Some may come from people who have evil intentions regarding us (*Psa.* 34:19–21). In addition, we have trouble with ourselves. Like Paul in Romans 7:24, we exclaim, 'Wretched man that I am! Who will deliver me from this body of death?'

SEEMING DEFEAT

Seventh, it often appears we are losing in the spiritual battle (v. 18). If we focus our attention on what is merely visible to the human eye, the battle in which we are engaged seems hopeless because the odds are so huge.

But we do not give up! Having identified grounds for discouragement, we are able to establish reasons for not giving up!

A SELF-AUTHENTICATING GOSPEL

First, although sadly there are many counterfeit gospels, our gospel – the ministry of the new covenant – is self-authenticating. We do not have to resort to underhand and shameful ways to get people to receive our message. We deliberately renounce such approaches. We do not use deception, and we do not distort God's Word. 'but by the open statement of the truth we would commend ourselves to everyone's conscience in the sight of God' (v. 2).

Behind this confidence is the hidden and all-powerful ministry of God the Holy Spirit, the Spirit of truth. No matter how difficult it may be for men and women to accept the truth about themselves as sinners – an acceptance the gospel message demands – God the Holy Spirit powerfully convicts them of its truth.

Full presentation of the truth receives the Spirit's full endorsement. As we declare the whole of the gospel, without compromise and without fear as to what men and women may say or do in reaction to it, we may rely upon the Spirit's power to make them recognise its truth.

GOD IS THE GOD OF SALVATION

Second, although we are involved in a spiritual battle with Satan, the god of this world, the God and Father of our Lord Jesus Christ, to whom we belong and whom we serve, is both the God of creation and the God

[45]

of salvation. While Satan blinds the minds of unbelievers so that they cannot see 'the light of the gospel of the glory of Christ, who is the image of God' (v. 4), 'God, who said, "Let light shine out of darkness"' nevertheless makes his light shine into people's hearts, as he has done in ours, to give them 'the light of the knowledge of the glory of God in the face of Jesus Christ' (v. 6).

New birth – or regeneration – is as dramatic and powerful a work as creation itself. It requires as great a power to shine into people's hearts to give spiritual understanding of Jesus' identity and work as it did to command light to shine out of darkness at the time of the creation. At new birth, men and women are made spiritually alive in Christ. God performs this miracle as the gospel – the new covenant – is preached. When we proclaim the gospel as we ought, we do not proclaim ourselves, but Jesus as Lord, and ourselves as other people's servants for Jesus' sake (v. 5). God then does his own unique and perfect work.

PURPOSE IN OUR WEAKNESS

Third, although we are marked by weakness and frailty, this is God's deliberate purpose so that it may be plain that the power is not ours but his! 'But we have this treasure in jars of clay, to show that the surpassing power belongs to God and not to us' (v. 7). This is another way of expressing the principle Paul established in 2 Corinthians 1:8–9: 'For we do not want you to be ignorant, brothers, of the affliction we experienced in Asia. For we were so utterly burdened beyond our strength that we despaired of life itself. Indeed, we felt that we had received the sentence of death. But that was to make us rely not on ourselves but on God who raises the dead.'

The theme of weakness runs through Paul's letters to the Corinthians and is prominent here. It is important to see ourselves as 'jars of clay' and not to have exaggerated views of our strength. Even those Christians whom we most admire for their godliness and gifts are just as much jars of clay as we are. God chooses to use such! He wants it to be obvious that the power of the gospel is not in its messengers but in its message about Jesus Christ our Lord.

THE ADEQUACY OF GOD'S GRACE

Fourth, although we are afflicted in a variety of ways, to the point that death may be said to be at work in us, God wonderfully has an answer for every situation. Although afflicted, we are not crushed (v. 8). He never allows us to be pressurised beyond what we can endure with his help. Perplexed at times, we are not in despair. We do not always know what to think or do or say, but we know and discover that God has the answers at the appropriate time. Sometimes persecuted, we are not forsaken (v. 9).

Difficult experiences bring precious proofs of Christ's presence (for example *2 Tim.* 4:17). Struck down, we are not destroyed (v. 9). We may lose a battle, but we do not lose the war! Identified with our Saviour in his death by our bitter experiences, we are wonderfully privileged to be identified with him in his resurrection power (v. 10). 'Death' experiences are followed by life! Furthermore, when we walk in our Saviour's footsteps, death in us brings life to others (v. 12). History illustrates and confirms that the blood of the martyrs is the seed of the church.

SPIRITUAL RENEWAL

Fifth, although we know the wear and tear of the spiritual battle, causing us to waste away, we know at the same time the spiritual miracle of inward renewal day by day (v. 16). This privilege is foreign to the experience of unbelieving men and women. We may find unique refreshment, even in extreme tiredness, when we know that we do God's will (see, for example, *John* 4:31–34). In the heat of the spiritual battle that the ministry of the new covenant involves, spiritual refreshment of the deepest sort may be known.

It may also be experienced when the wear and tear are at their height and most devastating. In Dr Martyn Lloyd-Jones' last days, his speech went from him. As one of his daughters, Elizabeth, sat beside him, 'he pointed her very definitely to the words of 2 Corinthians 4:16–18'. Elizabeth relates, 'When I asked him if that was his experience now, he nodded his head with great vigour' (I. H. Murray: *D.M. Lloyd-Jones*, Vol. II, p. 747).

ETERNAL GLORY OUTWEIGHS TROUBLES

Sixth, although we have troubles and will continue to do so, the eternal glory before us far outweighs them all. In comparison with that glory, our afflictions are light and momentary (v. 17). We would be dishonest if we did not admit to the reality of difficulties, but our testimony is that the Lord delivers the righteous from all their troubles (*Psa.* 34:19,21). The ultimate promise of deliverance from all our troubles is in the life to come, whereas for unbelievers their troubles then begin and never end (*Psa.* 34:19,21). Eternal glory is what our Saviour promises.

Our troubles work for our benefit as they prepare us for heaven. Sanctification is glory begun, and glory is sanctification completed. Glory equals the 'inheritance of the saints in light' (*Col.* 1:12; cf. 1:27). Glory will see the presentation of the bride, the church, to the bridegroom, our Lord Jesus Christ (*Col.* 1:22,28). The wonder of all that is before us in glory far outweighs all our troubles. Seen in the right perspective, all that now troubles us is little and transitory.

A RIGHT PERSPECTIVE

Finally, it may often appear that we are losing the spiritual battle, but that is to consider things from the wrong perspective (v. 18). If we employ the perspective of time alone, we may sometimes appear to be losing. When we consider things from an eternal perspective, however, we recognise we are on the winning side! Victory is already ours in our Saviour, because he has already gained it. God's saving purposes – through the ministry of the new covenant – are certain. So we 'look not to the things that are seen but to the things that are unseen. For the things that are seen are transient, but the things that are unseen are eternal' (v. 18).

THEREFORE!

'*So (therefore) we do not lose heart*' (v. 16; cf. v. 1). Balance is important here as elsewhere in our thinking. To engage in the ministry of the new covenant – another way of expressing evangelism – inevitably provokes opposition from Satan, and brings discouragements along the way. But we should turn our discouragements into encouragements. For every discouragement, God has a matching encouragement! Our blessings far outweigh our difficulties. The glories of our future in Christ more than compensate for present hardships. The key to the encouragement we need is fixing our eyes on the unseen, and supremely upon our unseen Saviour.

8

Our Heavenly Dwelling

¹For we know that if the tent that is our earthly home is destroyed, we have a building from God, a house not made with hands, eternal in the heavens. ²For in this tent we groan, longing to put on our heavenly dwelling, ³if indeed by putting it on we may not be found naked. ⁴For while we are still in this tent, we groan, being burdened—not that we would be unclothed, but that we would be further clothed, so that what is mortal may be swallowed up by life. ⁵He who has prepared us for this very thing is God, who has given us the Spirit as a guarantee.

⁶So we are always of good courage. We know that while we are at home in the body we are away from the Lord, ⁷for we walk by faith, not by sight. ⁸Yes, we are of good courage, and we would rather be away from the body and at home with the Lord. ⁹So whether we are at home or away, we make it our aim to please him. ¹⁰For we must all appear before the judgment seat of Christ, so that each one may receive what is due for what he has done in the body, whether good or evil (2 Cor. 5:1–10).

What sparked off this consideration of our 'eternal' house 'in the heavens' (v. 1) was Paul's explanation in the previous chapter of why the discouragements in gospel ministry do not cause us to lose heart.

Paul's final comments in chapter 4 focus upon the inner spiritual renewal we may experience, whatever may be happening to us outwardly or physically. He turns our eyes to the glory that is before us, now unseen, but eternal. It is in sharp contrast to the temporary and ephemeral things we see with our physical eyes. Verses 16 to

18 of chapter 4 present a glorious conclusion: 'So we do not lose heart. Though our outer self is wasting away, our inner self is being renewed day by day. For this light momentary affliction is preparing for us an eternal weight of glory beyond all comparison, as we look not to the things that are seen but to the things that are unseen. For the things that are seen are transient, but the things that are unseen are eternal.'

Essential to the glory before us is our resurrection body and heavenly home. Basic to our new birth is our living hope through the resurrection of our Lord Jesus from the dead. With it goes our assurance of a heavenly inheritance 'that is imperishable, undefiled, and unfading, kept in heaven' for us (*1 Pet.* 1:3–4).

THINGS WE KNOW

There are truths that, as Christians, we 'know' about our human body. *First, we know that our present body is but our earthly tent* (v. 1). Excellent though tents may be when we first obtain them and put them up, they are always of limited durability, especially when in constant use. They are subject to wear and tear in the storms from which they protect us. From the point of view of durability and fragility, our physical bodies are like tents.

Second, we know that our body's destiny is destruction (v. 1). Wonderful as the birth of a baby is, and perfect as its new body may seem to be, the seeds of death are already within it. We are born to live and then to die. We rightly speak of a lifespan, since life has both beginning and end. If the Lord Jesus does not return during our lifetime, our body, like a fragile tent, has a destiny to be destroyed, whether through natural decay or physical accident or danger (v. 1).

Third, we know, however, as believers, that our present earthly body is to be replaced by something much more wonderful, what Paul describes as 'our heavenly dwelling' (v. 2). It is not clear whether he has in view the resurrection body God promises, or the sphere – heaven – in which we will live out our new life in our resurrection bodies.

These three truths we know because God promises them. They are crucial to our heavenly inheritance in our Saviour. As believers, we are people of hope, 'sons of the resurrection' (*Luke* 20:36).

WITH KNOWLEDGE GOES TENSION

Our longings for the glory promised us, coupled with present discouragements in our service of the gospel, often cause us to 'groan' (v. 2). 'For while we are still in this tent, we groan, being burdened' (v. 4). We are painfully aware that so much of what is true of us now is so different from what is in glorious prospect. Being burdened is characteristic of us while we are in this body. The body is rather like an old car with which all sorts of different things keep going wrong.

While in our present human body, we discover many grounds for frustration, as we long to be clothed with our resurrection bodies in heaven (v. 2). The prospect of glory increases our desire to put off this earthly tent – our physical body. We want to do so, not just because of our body's inherent weakness and accompanying problems, but because of the wonder of what is going to replace it.

GLORIFICATION

In heaven we will be clothed with our heavenly dwelling. 'The Lord Jesus Christ . . . will transform our lowly body to be like his glorious body, by the power that enables him even to subject all things to himself' (*Phil.* 3:20–21). What is mortal is going to be 'swallowed up by life' (v. 4). The expression 'swallowed up' points to the dramatic nature of the change. Paul has in prospect our glorification, something for which spiritually healthy Christians increasingly long.

Glorification is the term used to describe Christians' ultimate complete conformity to the image of our Lord Jesus Christ. This glorious work that will take place at his coming (*Col.* 3:4, *1 John* 3:2). It is the logical outcome of predestination, calling and justification, a consequence so certain that it can be described as having already taken place (*Rom.* 8:30). 'My thoughts, and the deepest places of my soul are torn with every kind of tumult until the day when I shall be purified and melted in the fire of Your love, and wholly joined to You,' Augustine declared. 'God . . . has made us for this very purpose' (v. 5). He redeemed us with this glorious end in view.

THE HOLY SPIRIT, THE GUARANTEE

The guarantee of this wonderful prospect is the Holy Spirit given to every believer (v. 5). This picture of the guarantee or deposit is worthy of exploration, since it helps us to understand an important aspect of his ministry. Through familiarity it is possible to overlook the greatness of God's generosity in the gift of the Spirit. He is the Third Person of the Trinity, and he possesses all the attributes of God. He lives within us as believers and makes our bodies his temple. Without his indwelling, we would not be God's children. Without his living within us, we would not possess spiritual life.

That he lives in us, however, is the proof and promise of what God is yet going to give us. Having begun a good work in us, he guarantees its completion (*Phil.*1:6), and his Holy Spirit is the divine workman. The Spirit prepares us for glory. Even as the Spirit raised our Lord Jesus from the dead, so he will raise our bodies. The Spirit witnesses to us that glory is our home, and that where our Saviour is, we now belong. This provides a tremendous ground for encouragement, no matter how fierce may be the spiritual battle with the god of this world, or how many the difficulties we face as we proclaim the gospel of our Saviour.

KNOWLEDGE AND CONFIDENCE

We have already identified truths we know about our human existence and our heavenly destiny. We possess, however, both knowledge and courage, or *confidence* (v. 6). Courage and confidence spring from knowledge. We have sure grounds to be confident because of what we clearly know.

We *know* that as long as we are at home in the body we are away from the Lord (v. 6). We cannot be in two places at once! While alive in this world we cannot be at the same time in heaven.

Our confident assurance concerning the future means we would prefer to be away from the body and to be at home with the Lord. Paul's opening up of his heart's desires to the Philippians explains what he means. He writes, 'For to me to live is Christ, and to die is gain. If I am to live in the flesh, that means fruitful labour for me. Yet which I shall choose I cannot tell. I am hard pressed between the two. My desire is to depart and be with Christ, for that is far better. But to remain in the flesh is more necessary on your account.' (*Phil.* 1:21–24). His words here in 2 Corinthians 5 and Philippians 1 point to the immediate presence of a Christian's soul with the Lord Jesus at the moment of death. The New Testament assumes that death means conscious entry at once into the Lord's presence – to be at home with him. 'At home with the Lord' (v. 8) is a delightful expression. When we are away from home, we long to be just there! Home for the Christian is where Jesus is.

FAITH, NOT SIGHT, IS THE PRINCIPLE BY WHICH WE LIVE

We cannot see our heavenly home. We cannot see our Saviour, the Lord Jesus. We cannot see the glory that is before us. God-given faith, nurtured by the Holy Spirit, however, makes us increasingly more sure of the unseen than of the seen. This reminds us of our Saviour's words, such as 'Let not your hearts be troubled. Believe in God; believe also in me. In my Father's house are many rooms. If it were not so, would I have told you that I go to prepare a place for you?' (*John* 14:1–2). He encourages us to live in the light of such a promise. Although we cannot see our Saviour, the Holy Spirit makes us so sure of him that we 'rejoice with joy that is inexpressible and filled with glory' (*1 Pet.* 1:8). As Moses did, we may persevere because with another kind of sight altogether we see him who is invisible (*Heb.* 11:27). Although our physical eyes cannot now see the promised glory, the Holy Spirit teaches us that sanctification is glory begun as we become more and more like the Lord Jesus in life and character (*2 Cor.* 3:18). This ability to live by faith, and not by sight, provides another explanation for our not being overcome by discouragement as we exercise the ministry of the new covenant.

OUR PROPER GOAL

When we live by faith with the prospect of eternal glory, one ambition alone is appropriate: 'whether we are at home or away, we make it our aim to please him' (v. 9). Before we were believers, we had either no ambitions or perhaps too many, with most motivated by human selfishness. As Christians we ought to be ambitious – ambitious to please our Lord and Master. Paul made this his aim.

As we recall our conversion, we recognise how radically our ambitions changed. We may not have appreciated their revolutionary nature at the time, but there was no doubt about it. Our new sense of indebtedness to God and awareness of our Saviour's grace produce a gratitude that shows itself in determination to please the Lord. Life is simplified because we know that to please him puts everything else in its proper place. For us to live has become Christ (*Phil.* 1:21).

The certainty of the coming judgment underlines the wisdom of this determination. 'For we must all appear before the judgment seat of Christ, so that each one may receive what is due for what he has done in the body, whether good or evil' (*2 Cor.* 5:10).

The One who will judge all human beings is our Lord Jesus, and the judgment seat is his (v. 10). While, as believers, our salvation at the judgment is not in doubt, our receiving of our Saviour's 'Well done, good and faithful servant' may be. Each of us will receive what is due for the things we have done in the body, whether good or bad (v. 10). Our body is the sphere in which we now live and do either good or evil. It is the instrument by which we may honour the Lord Jesus (*Phil.* 1:20). We shall be judged therefore for the use of our body and its energies. The doctrine of careful and exact retribution is plainly taught throughout the Bible, as here.

The key issue at the judgment for every one will be the possession of faith in the Lord Jesus and the new covenant. The key issue for all who have entered the new covenant through faith in him will be their obedience to the stewardship of that new covenant. Only one thing guarantees our hearing our Master's 'Well done' (*Matt.* 25:21,23): making it daily our ambition to please him.

9

Continuance in the Task of Evangelism

¹¹Therefore, knowing the fear of the Lord, we persuade others. But what we are is known to God, and I hope it is known also to your conscience. ¹²We are not commending ourselves to you again but giving you cause to boast about us, so that you may be able to answer those who boast about outward appearance and not about what is in the heart. ¹³For if we are beside ourselves, it is for God; if we are in our right mind, it is for you. ¹⁴For the love of Christ controls us, because we have concluded this: that one has died for all, therefore all have died; ¹⁵and he died for all, that those who live might no longer live for themselves but for him who for their sake died and was raised.

¹⁶From now on, therefore, we regard no one according to the flesh. Even though we once regarded Christ according to the flesh, we regard him thus no longer. ¹⁷Therefore, if anyone is in Christ, he is a new creation. The old has passed away; behold, the new has come. ¹⁸All this is from God, who through Christ reconciled us to himself and gave us the ministry of reconciliation; ¹⁹that is, in Christ God was reconciling the world to himself, not counting their trespasses against them, and entrusting to us the message of reconciliation. ²⁰Therefore, we are ambassadors for Christ, God making his appeal through us. We implore you on behalf of Christ, be reconciled to God. ²¹For our sake he made him to be sin who knew no sin, so that in·him we might become the righteousness of God (2 Cor. 5:11–21).

One theme is continually present in 2 Corinthians. It is always below the surface, and sometimes it comes to the fore, as here. It is the many-faceted explanation of why Paul does not give up in the spiritual battle that evangelism involves. We have seen already, for example, that God's mercy in the Lord Jesus continually spurred him on (4:1). He has just been underlining the living and glorious hope the Lord Jesus gives us of heaven and resurrection life. That confidence gives backbone to evangelism. He now shares other underlying grounds for his commitment to the task. This passage is vital to any consideration of biblical evangelism.

THE FEAR OF GOD

Paul begins with the fear of the Lord (v. 11). 'Therefore, knowing the fear the Lord.' That arises from our knowing that 'we must all appear before the judgment seat of Christ, so that each one may receive what is due for what he has done in the body, whether good or evil' (v. 10). Since the gospel is the most precious gift God has entrusted to us, accountability for our stewardship of it must clearly figure in our Saviour's judgment upon our life and service.

The thought of judgment immediately creates a sense of awe and reverence. The judgment our Saviour will execute is divine judgment, and we know that it is awesome and perfect. True knowledge therefore prompts us to behave seriously. Our highest wisdom is to live our life now with an eye to that future judgment, and that will make us aware of our responsibility for the souls of all those close to us and around us.

When we are aware of the coming judgment, and our accountability for ourselves and the spiritual well-being of others, we 'persuade others' (v. 11). Evangelism is not something to be engaged in without feeling and passion. In sharing the gospel, we deal with the basic issue of life or death, of eternal salvation or eternal condemnation. Evangelism inevitably contains therefore an important element of persuasion. Using the key weapon of truth – the Scriptures – we try to persuade men and women of the truth of the gospel and of their urgent need to respond to it (cf. *Acts* 18:4; 28:23).

Persuasion, however, must be done with integrity. We will not engage in the persuasion we may occasionally encounter of a crafty telephone or door-to-door sales person. Paul renounced such approaches (*2 Cor.* 4: 2). Paul appeals to the Corinthians' personal knowledge and acquaintance of his colleagues and himself: 'what we are is known to God, and I hope it is known also to your conscience' (v. 11). Paul hoped that the Corinthians could bear witness to their integrity.

The fragility of Paul's relationship to the Corinthians surfaces again here. He felt that he must not appear to be trying to commend himself and his friends to them. Rather, he wanted to provide an opportunity for the Corinthians to take pride in them, so that they had answers to give to any who took pride in unworthy things. However, whatever his readers or others thought, Paul knew that God knows the truth about us (v. 11), and godliness concerns itself with his evaluation rather than human opinions.

Paul was plainly aware of criticisms levelled against him and his fellow missionaries, many of which may have been contradictory. Some accused them of being out of their right mind (v. 13), probably because of their uncompromising obedience to the Lord Jesus' last commission. Paul's answer was that their motive in whatever they did was to do it for God's sake and the good of their hearers (v. 13).

In a world that does not take seriously God's holiness and righteousness, any proclamation of divine judgment will be regarded by some as madness. If judgment is not understood or accepted, then there will be no awareness of the need for salvation. The gospel is then viewed as irrelevant or utter foolishness. Enthusiasm for the gospel will often be thought madness by the world. However, we are not unhappy at such accusations if we are sure that what prompts them are our integrity, obedience to God and concern for men and women's souls.

To fear God is to reverence him as the God and Father of our Lord Jesus Christ and to aim to please him above all other goals. To know the fear of God is to be committed to the spread of the good news.

THE COMPULSION OF CHRIST'S LOVE

Along with the fear of God as a gospel motive goes the constraint of Christ's love. 'For the love of Christ controls us' (v. 14). No matter what the opposition or physical difficulties, the early missionaries found themselves driven to fulfil his commission by the power of their Saviour's love. They were sure of his love for them and his love for those with whom they shared the good news. The love of the Lord Jesus Christ is a rich treasure we both know and yet recognise is beyond our knowledge because it is so vast and immeasurable.

Paul quickly indicates the high point of the revelation we have of Christ's love. 'We have concluded this: that one has died for all, therefore all have died' (v. 14). Paul understood how widespread were the effects and consequences of that single death of the Lord Jesus. He knew it was for the innumerable company of those who would enjoy the benefits of his eternal redemption. It marked the death of all, in that he died the death they all should have died. Their penalty was borne by him as he died in their place. All this happened before ever they thought of him or loved him – while they were his enemies.

Fundamental to the convictions that motivated the apostles and early missionaries was the substitutionary death of our Lord Jesus Christ. His death was the reason for everything that they did. Their lives, like the lives of all Christians, were built upon the solid truth that Jesus died for us and was raised again (v. 15). As a consequence they knew that they could no longer live for themselves, but rather had to live for his sake with a sense of profound indebtedness and gratitude (v. 15). There is a 'no longer' element about every genuine Christian life. We can no longer live for ourselves, but we must live for him – not grudgingly, but with a deep sense of privilege. Our Saviour's foremost concern is the gathering in of his lost sheep, for whom he died. To live for him, therefore, is to share his concern for them and to be committed to making known his gospel.

THE DIVINE WORK OF REGENERATION

Basic to any understanding of new covenant ministry or evangelism is the foundation truth that the work is essentially God's. We may be co-workers, but the real work is his. From beginning to end, new birth is 'from God' (v. 18).

The gospel is all about the new covenant. We enter into that new covenant through new birth, or regeneration. Paul sums that work up in verse 17: 'Therefore, if anyone is in Christ, he is a new creation. the old has passed away; behold, the new has come.'

Becoming a Christian is here defined as being 'in Christ'. As God brings us to repentance and faith in his Son through the gospel, he performs the work of new birth in us by his Spirit. We are united spiritually to Jesus Christ, so that all that he accomplished by his death and resurrection becomes ours. We receive the forgiveness of our sins and a new start.

The work of new birth is totally uninfluenced by our human status or lack of it. Consequently, when we understand the new covenant, we do not assess people any more by what they look like or by what they possess. (Paul mentions in passing that this was the reason he and his fellow Jews got it all wrong when they looked at Jesus, the Messiah, in a purely human way – v. 16.) When it comes to new birth and entry into the new covenant, it does not matter whether we are Jews or Gentiles, black or white, rich or poor. Hence Paul writes, 'From now on, therefore, we regard no one according to the flesh' (v. 16). New birth is a work of 'new creation', 'the old has passed away . . . the new has come.' (v. 17).

Nothing is more exciting than witnessing new birth taking place, and all the glorious changes that flow from it. As we play our part in sharing the gospel, God uses it to bring men and women to spiritual new birth. That is one of the best of encouragements to keep going!

THE MOST IMPORTANT ENCOURAGEMENT IS THE GOSPEL ITSELF

This gospel is from God. Simple though that statement is, it says so much. 'All this is from God . . .' (v. 18). From him comes the gospel of reconciliation. The theme of reconciliation is dominant in the remaining verses of this passage. The basic statement is that 'God . . . through Christ reconciled us to himself' (v. 18). The crux of that reconciling work was his 'not counting (men's) trespasses against them' (v. 19). Reconciliation, in essence, means that God, through Christ, does not impute our trespasses any longer to us. The opposite of his counting our sins to us, as we deserve, is his blotting out our sins. How God achieved this is succinctly and wonderfully expressed: 'he made him to be sin who knew no sin, so that in him we might become the righteousness of God' (v. 21).

Our Lord Jesus Christ's sinlessness was crucial to our forgiveness and salvation. Because he knew no sin, he could take ours. The gospel is the good news of the great exchange. That exchange took place at the cross. The Lord Jesus took in our place the wrath of God our sins deserve, so that, in exchange, we might receive his righteousness.

Besides the gift of perfect and eternal salvation, another consequence immediately follows. Reconciled to God, we become Christ's ambassadors in the world. All who are reconciled to God are entrusted with the message of reconciliation (v. 19). Crucial to our being ambassadors is that God makes his appeal to others through us (v. 20). That makes sense, because as we look back on our own conversion and new birth, most of us can see how God used Christian people to speak to us in his name.

Rightly understood, in evangelism it is God himself who makes the appeal. We are to implore men and women, 'Be reconciled to God' (v. 20). We are to urge them to find their peace with him through the provision he has made for sinners in his Son's death. As we do so, it is God's voice that they hear and recognise. What greater privilege can there be in life?

The more we understand the gospel and its glories, the more privileged we know ourselves to be in sharing it with others. We are not all called to be evangelists and pastors and teachers. However, we are all called to be ready to explain the hope that is ours in our Lord Jesus Christ (*1 Pet.* 3:15).

When we put together the wonder of the gospel itself, our fear of God, the compulsion of our Saviour's love, and the certainty of the miracle of new birth accompanying the preaching of the good news, we find we have every encouragement to continue, just as Paul and his colleagues did!

Honouring the Ministry of the New Covenant

¹Working together with him, then, we appeal to you not to receive the grace of God in vain. ²For he says,

> *'In a favorable time I listened to you,*
> *and in a day of salvation I have helped you.'*

Behold, now is the favorable time; behold, now is the day of salvation. ³We put no obstacle in anyone's way, so that no fault may be found with our ministry, ⁴but as servants of God we commend ourselves in every way: by great endurance, in afflictions, hardships, calamities, ⁵beatings, imprisonments, riots, labours, sleepless nights, hunger; ⁶by purity, knowledge, patience, kindness, the Holy Spirit, genuine love; ⁷by truthful speech, and the power of God; with the weapons of righteousness for the right hand and for the left; ⁸through honour and dishonour, through slander and praise. We are treated as impostors, and yet are true; ⁹as unknown, and yet well known; as dying, and behold, we live; as punished, and yet not killed; ¹⁰as sorrowful, yet always rejoicing; as poor, yet making many rich; as having nothing, yet possessing everything.

¹¹We have spoken freely to you, Corinthians; our heart is wide open. ¹²You are not restricted by us, but you are restricted in your own affections. ¹³In return (I speak as to children) widen your hearts also (2 Cor. 6:1–13).

It is difficult to know whether to put verses 1 and 2 of chapter 6 with the end of chapter 5 or with the first section of chapter 6 beginning at verse 3. They provide a bridge between the two parts. Paul has shared in 5:11–21 the wonder of the gospel in its achievement and declaration of God's reconciling work through the atoning death of his Son.

The Corinthians knew the gospel well, for they had received it from Paul himself (*Acts* 18:11, *1 Cor.* 15:1–8). They had realised that when Paul and his colleagues proclaimed this good news that it was the 'day of salvation' for them (v. 2). It was the time when they personally could call upon God for the salvation he promises in his Son. They called, and he heard them: they were saved. It is in his grace that God hears us and in the day of salvation that he helps us (v. 2). This the Corinthians knew.

Knowing, however, is not sufficient. God's grace is to be 'received' and received effectively – that is to say, not 'in vain'. We receive God's grace so that it does its work in us.

A KEY QUESTION

It is important to ask, therefore, 'What is it "to receive the grace of God in vain"?' (v. 1) We find the answer as we recognise the relationship between grace and gratitude. To receive God's grace in vain is to fail to respond with the gratitude that demands we live the rest of our lives in glad obedience to God (cf. *2 Cor.* 5:15). The fitting response to grace is gratitude. Significantly, the same Greek word expresses both words. In Christianity, theology is grace and ethics is gratitude.

Gratitude should be a distinguishing feature of us as Christians throughout our life. Growing and built up in the Lord Jesus and strengthened in our God-given faith, we should overflow with thankfulness to God (*Col.* 2:7). Gratitude is one of our healthiest emotions. When, for example, we read the opening verses of Psalm 103, gratitude shines out in every line. It is the sum and total duty of the Christian. If we live gratefully to God for his Son, then we live holily. We impoverish our spiritual life if we live ungratefully.

The human heart does not easily sustain and maintain gratitude. Our memories are all too short. One reason for the establishing of the Lord's Supper, and our need to meet regularly around his Table, is to stir anew our memories of his grace, so that we determine to live thankfully. Grace leading to gratitude destroys our natural disposition to resist God. It causes us to delight in his law as never before. It is a major motive for service of the Lord Jesus. Paul's appeal to the Corinthians not to receive God's grace in vain is therefore just as relevant to us. The evidence of its reception is that it does its work in us.

AMBASSADORS' LIVES MUST COMMEND THEIR MESSAGE

Paul has identified himself and his colleagues as 'ambassadors for Christ' (*2 Cor.* 5:20), a title we may take in some measure to ourselves, since the apostolic gospel has been entrusted to us. In urging the Corinthians 'not to receive the grace of God in vain', Paul and his fellow missionaries fulfilled their ambassadorial function 'working together with him'. They declared what they knew their Master wanted their hearers to hear.

The NIV gives verses 3 to 13 the heading *Paul's Hardships*, but for two reasons this is not the best title. First, Paul uses the word 'we' (v. 3), so what he writes does not refer only to him. Second, his concern in what he writes is not for himself but for the esteem in which the ministry of the new covenant should be held (v. 3). He writes of 'our ministry' because God had committed it to him and his companions; but the gospel is *God's* gospel, and the ministry of the new covenant is both the gift and work of God.

The ministry of the new covenant vitally involves God's name and honour, just as the behaviour of ambassadors is intimately connected to their nation's reputation and esteem. It is difficult, if not impossible, to separate the preaching of the gospel from the lives and conduct of those who proclaim it. Our conduct reflects – for good or bad – upon the good news we proclaim. By the way we live we are to 'adorn the doctrine of God our Saviour' (*Titus* 2:10).

The quality of life of God's representatives should recommend God to the world. Paul probably never forgot the effect that Stephen's blamelessness, under the severest of trials, had upon him as he observed it (*Acts* 7:54–60). 'Not to receive the grace of God in vain' is to live so that our lives provide living testimonials to the gospel's power. This principle is behind Paul's appeal at the beginning of chapter 6. In the verses that follow he explains what this means.

CONDUCT THAT HONOURS CHRIST AND THE GOSPEL

Paul's teaching summarises conduct that honours the ministry of the new covenant in seven ways.

First, it means putting no obstacle in anyone's path. 'We put no obstacle in anyone's way, so that no fault may be found with our ministry' (v. 3). Unconverted men and women often try to find excuses for not believing the gospel. A common excuse is the inconsistent behaviour of those who profess to be Christians. Christians, too, may shrug off the plain teaching of the Bible if their teachers are not an example of what they teach. Being aware of this problem helps us to avoid it. Our Lord Jesus gave particular warning to those who put such hindrances in the path of children (*Matt.* 18:6).

Second, conduct that honours Christ and the gospel demands that we prove ourselves as those who endure – that is to say, that we are overcomers. Endurance means overcoming afflictions, hardships, calamities, beatings, imprisonments, labours, sleepless nights or hunger (vv. 4–5). In providing this list, Paul indicates some of the experiences he and his companions knew. Endurance is a consistent New Testament theme and demand of discipleship (*Rom.* 15:4, *1 Cor.* 4:12, *Col.* 1:11, *2 Tim.* 2:3, 10, 12; 4:5, *Heb.* 12:7, *Rev.* 3:10). The peril when faced with such difficulties is to collapse, to give in, and to retreat. To endure is not only to see these challenges through to their satisfactory conclusion, but to do so without grumbling or bitterness – in other words, to respond to grace with gratitude.

Third, conduct that honours Christ and the gospel must be marked by purity (v. 6). Part of fundamental and elementary ethical teaching for new Christians is that God's will is that we should be sanctified. Sanctification includes avoiding sexual immorality and learning to control our body in a way that is holy and honourable (*1 Thess.* 4:3).

Sadly, experience proves that one of the most subtle ways in which the enemy of souls brings dishonour to Christ and the gospel is through the moral – and often sexual – indiscretions and sins of those who proclaim it. We should not be surprised at this, since it is the area of greatest human vulnerability. However, this does not excuse it, and gratitude, responding to grace, prompts us to be all the more determined to be on our guard and to make no excuses for lack of watchfulness. Practical purity demands purity of motive and intention. When in evangelism or counselling we find ourselves wanting to deal with those of the opposite sex, or we find ourselves becoming particularly close to them, alarm bells should ring. We should then take immediate evasive and preventative action. To suggest we do not need to do so only shows us to be more vulnerable than we choose to admit.

Fourth, conduct that honours Christ and the gospel is marked by knowledge, patience, kindness and love in the Spirit's power (v. 6). Paul does not define the 'knowledge' he has in view. Its position between 'purity' and 'patience' implies 'knowledge' of priorities and of people. Such perception is part of the Holy Spirit's work in us. Patience, kindness and love are aspects of his fruit in our lives (*Gal.* 5:22). In all our dealings with others, we are to reflect and portray the character of the Lord Jesus.

Fifth, conduct that honours Christ and the gospel requires truthful speech (v. 7). If people are to believe the testimony we give to the new covenant, they must be able to believe what we say about everything else. They will judge the truthfulness of the gospel by what they know already about our truthfulness. They will assess the honesty of God's promises by our honesty. The God and Father of our Lord Jesus Christ is the God of truth, and truthfulness in all its forms must mark us.

Sixth, conduct that honours Christ and the gospel requires dependence upon God's power, especially in the use of the weapons of righteousness (v. 7). We can achieve nothing of lasting worth without God's energy and strength. We cannot wage spiritual warfare with merely human resources. As the Lord Jesus taught, without him we cannot do anything of worth (*John* 15:5). When the world talks of weapons, it usually thinks of visible human assets and weapons of human prestige or esteem. The weapons we are to use in dependence on God's power are 'weapons of righteousness for the right hand and for the left' (v. 7). This is another way of saying that whatever we do, without any possible exception, we must concentrate on doing what is right in God's sight. We are not to do simply what is humanly expedient or astute. Rather we are to ask, 'What is right in God's sight according to the teaching of his Word and the application of its principles?'

When we honestly ask such a question, God the Holy Spirit, the Spirit of truth, guides us to the right answer. As we follow his direction, we have in one hand his sword, the Scriptures, and in the other, the shield of faith, a shield we raise every time we ask God for help to do what is right. The use of these weapons is to be maintained 'through honour and dishonour, through slander and praise', whether we are regarded as genuine or impostors, whether we are recognised by the world or ignored by it (vv. 8–9). Our strategy as we fulfil the ministry of the new covenant is not to be worldly-wise or political, but spiritual and Christ-honouring.

Sometimes Paul's reputation stood high, while at other times he was viewed as of no account and treated with contempt. He was both defamed and praised, criticised and appreciated. Such experiences come to all who walk in Jesus' footsteps, serving as his representatives and ambassadors.

Finally, conduct that honours Christ and the gospel requires the willingness to live for the sake of others (vv. 9–10). Some may face death for the gospel. Others may be 'punished, and yet not killed' (v. 9). We may be 'sorrowful, yet always rejoicing' (v. 10). We may make 'many rich, as having nothing, yet possessing everything' (v. 10). Such a lifestyle is eminently reasonable when we live with the assurance Paul gives at the end of chapter 4, 'For this light momentary affliction is preparing for us an eternal weight of glory beyond all comparison, as we look not to the things that are seen but to the things that are unseen. For the things that are seen are transient, but the things that are unseen are eternal' (vv. 17–18).

OPEN HEARTEDNESS

In writing so honestly, Paul and his colleagues kept nothing back of their feelings (v. 11). This direct approach arose from their affection for the Corinthians (v. 12). Paul longed that they would reciprocate. Again, we can feel the somewhat tense relationship between them. When we become aware that people are reticent, and perhaps unwilling to open up to us, the best way forward often is to open up ourselves to them, rather than simply grumbling and regarding it as a lost cause. That may make us feel very vulnerable, especially if they reject us even more. Nevertheless, it is the path of love and   the kind of behaviour that honours the Lord Jesus and the new covenant.

In the World but Not of It

¹⁴Do not be unequally yoked with unbelievers. For what partnership has righteousness with lawlessness? Or what fellowship has light with darkness? ¹⁵What accord has Christ with Belial? Or what portion does a believer share with an unbeliever? ¹⁶What agreement has the temple of God with idols? For we are the temple of the living God; as God said,

> *'I will make my dwelling among them and walk among them,*
> *and I will be their God,*
> *and they shall be my people.*
> *¹⁷Therefore go out from their midst,*
> *and be separate from them, says the Lord,*
> *and touch no unclean thing;*
> *then I will welcome you,*
> *¹⁸and I will be a father to you,*
> *and you shall be sons and daughters to me,*
> *says the Lord Almighty.'*

¹Since we have these promises, beloved, let us cleanse ourselves from every defilement of body and spirit, bringing holiness to completion in the fear of God (2 Cor. 6:14–7:1).

Paul turns to an area of pastoral concern. It is clearly part of what he had in mind when he wrote about not receiving the grace of God in vain (v. 1).

God intends the *experience* of salvation to follow the *gift* of salvation. Isaiah declares, 'Behold, God is my salvation; I will trust, and will not be afraid; for the Lord God is my strength and my song, and he has become my salvation' (*Isa.* 12:2). To be saved means here understanding the truth about God, putting our fears to flight, and so discovering God's strength and joy that a song is upon our lips.

Salvation is not God's occasional act. Rather it is one of his attributes, since he is the saving God. Three tenses of salvation are always present in the New Testament. We have been saved (*Eph.* 2:8), in that when we believed on the Lord Jesus Christ we were freed from the guilt and penalty of sin. We are also being saved at this present time, in that we are delivered from sin's power (*1 Cor.* 1:18). Furthermore, we will be saved because at our Saviour's coming we are to be delivered even from the presence of sin for ever (*Rom.* 5:9, *Phil.* 3:21). In Paul's letter to the Romans, the verb 'to save' is significantly in the future tense on seven of its eight occurrences. Part of the present experience of salvation is our deliverance from the world's pressures upon us to compromise our faith in, and our loyalty to, our Lord Jesus Christ. Paul relates himself now to a challenge we all know.

IDENTIFYING THE PROBLEM

The problem is the proper relationship of Christians to non-Christians, especially with regard to marriage and business partnerships. None of the Corinthians had been Christians for long. They were comparatively young in the faith. They probably all had unconverted family members. In daily work they rubbed shoulders with unbelieving colleagues. They lived among neighbours and friends who were not Christians. How close to them should their relationship be?

The question is always relevant because we do become different people in many respects at new birth. As Paul has written in the previous chapter, 'Therefore, if anyone is in Christ, he is a new creation; the old has passed away; behold, the new has come' (*2 Cor.* 5:17).

The change in many of the Corinthians had been dramatic. In his first letter Paul asked, 'do you not know that the unrighteous will not inherit the kingdom of God?' Having asked the question, he continues, 'Do not be deceived: neither the sexually immoral, nor idolaters, nor adulterers, nor men who practice homosexuality, nor thieves, nor the greedy, nor drunkards, nor revilers, nor swindlers will inherit the kingdom of God.' Then he makes a telling statement: 'And such *were* some of you. But you were washed, you were sanctified, you were justified in the name of the Lord Jesus Christ and by the Spirit of our God.' (*1 Cor.* 6:9–11, italics added).

Because of our union with the Lord Jesus Christ, we do not belong to the world as once we did (*Col.* 2:20). We march to a different drum. We live our lives to another agenda. Nevertheless, we still continue to live in the world. To do so without it affecting us adversely is not easy. It is as hard to live in the world and to be unaffected by it as it is to go swimming without getting wet or to work in a garden without getting dirty. The world's mindset focuses upon the physical and the sexual rather than the spiritual and the holy. Living in the world is like existing in an atmosphere where there is always danger of contagion with deadly disease. However, it is not God's present purpose to take us out of the world, or for us to ignore the people around us. The opposite is the case. We have a duty and privilege to witness to the world and to win men and women for the Lord Jesus Christ.

If we are in the world and not of it, but committed to bearing testimony to Jesus Christ in it, how close should our relationship to the world be? That is the crucial question. Our association must be real, otherwise we cannot function properly as salt and light. Meat in first-century Corinth was not saved from corruption by withdrawing the presence of salt from it. We do not relieve the world's darkness by removing light from it.

INEVITABLE TENSIONS

'Do not be unequally yoked with unbelievers' (v. 14) is Paul's exhortation. 'Yoked' is a term associated with animals. It might be used of oxen as they ploughed a field in harness. It speaks of a close association or involvement, a partnership of the closest kind.

Intimate partnership with men and women of the world is impossible because of four inevitable tensions. *First, there is the tension between righteousness and lawlessness* (v. 14). The practical outcome of Christians' relationship to the one true and righteous

God is that they must be committed to doing what is right, whatever the cost and without argument. That is not to suggest that unconverted men and women may not strive to do what is right. However, they are not likely to make it their top priority. Self-interest and expediency may sometimes overrule it.

Second, there is the tension between light and darkness (v. 14). God is light, and the Lord Jesus Christ spoke of himself as the light of the world (*John* 8:12). To live in fellowship with God is to 'walk in the light, as he is in the light' (*1 John* 1:7). Born into God's family, Christians find God's light cast upon their path. We see clearly the way God wants us to go if we are to live in harmony with him. If not born again, however, men and women's minds are darkened by sin and dominated by the ruler of darkness, the devil, as once we were.

Third, there is the tension between Christ and Belial (v. 15). 'Belial' is a word found frequently in the Old Testament. Its original meaning was either worthlessness or hopeless ruin. In the period between the Old and New Testaments it became a name for Satan, the devil. Christians, having been rescued from the domain of darkness and transferred to the kingdom of God's Son (*Col.* 1:13), are plainly on Christ's side and opposed to Satan's works. Men and women of the world, without their knowing it, are under Satan's domination.

Fourth, there is the tension between God's temple and idols (v. 16). Devotion to a divinity in the first century expressed itself in loyalty to the temple or shrine of the god where people worshipped. The understanding Christians have of worship is different from that possessed by unconverted men and women. The gospel of the new covenant reveals that God's temple is not a material building of wood and stone. Rather his people, of whom God makes living stones, are his spiritual temple that he inhabits by his Spirit. Men and women of the world imagine their gods – so called – to be associated with places, where dishonourable practices are sometimes performed as part of the worship. The two ideas – one true and the other false – are in complete opposition.

These four tensions hang together, since they are all aspects of the difference between the once-born and the twice-born. While as Christians we share many things with unbelievers, the things we do not and cannot share make 'partnership' impossible without compromise.

MARRIAGE AND BUSINESS

Traditionally the main application of this passage has been to marriage. That is correct, since we find the same principles established elsewhere in the Bible (*e.g.*, *1 Cor.* 7:39). To be successful, marriage requires both partners to share their basic interests. For Christians, the most important part of life is their relationship to God through Jesus Christ. Not to be able to share the joys and privileges of that relationship with a marriage partner sows seeds of potential division rather than of unity. More important, it dishonours God, since he deserves first place in our affections. The 'love (we) had at first' (*Rev.* 2:4) for our Master is the minimum priority of our lives. Problems inevitably arise when Christians are unequally yoked in marriage. Many surround the upbringing of children and the role model parents should provide.

The application of 'yoked', however, is wider than marriage. It is unfortunate and unhelpful that we have often limited it to that. We must apply the test to other binding partnerships such as in business and commerce. Many directors or bosses of a business can bear witness to the tensions that their conversion has brought with non-Christian partners. While in business profit predominates as a motive, for the Christian it cannot be the overruling motive if moral standards and convictions are at stake. As in the case of marriage, the suggestion is not that a newly converted boss or business partner should immediately sever the partnership. That would be dishonourable, and such a decision may not always be the right way forward. It is vitally important too to apply this principle in a manner consistent with others in the Bible, such as our duty to function as salt in the world. In professions that operate through partnerships, a partnership is often the way promotion is offered, as management roles may be in other businesses. The promotion involved may be a God-given opportunity to make a Christian contribution where it is vitally needed. However, we need to beware of *initiating* or *entering into* partnerships where high moral values are not shared and where our Christian witness may be compromised. This principle applies to involvement and membership of organisations contrary to the gospel in belief and practice.

OUR NEW IDENTITY

'We are the temple of the living God' (v. 16). Having spotlighted the problem, Paul reminds the Corinthians of our new identity as God's temple. The significance of this description of God's people is considerable. It is hardly possible to exaggerate the importance of the temple to the Jews. There, uniquely, God was expected to be present and worshipped in holiness.

Fundamental to spiritual understanding, however, is that no temple made by human hands can ever contain God or be a fitting home for him. Both David and Solomon recognised this. The New Testament goes further and reveals that God is building a new temple, although not one made of bricks or stones from the earth's natural resources. The foundation upon which this temple is built is the Lord Jesus Christ, 'a cornerstone chosen and precious' (*1 Pet.* 2:6). He is the 'living stone rejected by men but in the sight of God chosen and precious' (*1 Pet.* 2:4). As we put our trust in the Lord Jesus Christ as the Son of God and Saviour, we receive spiritual   life and like living stones or bricks, are built into God's new temple. Made also spiritual priests in that temple, we are able to offer 'spiritual sacrifices acceptable to God through Jesus Christ' (*1 Pet.* 2:5). The key issue regarding God's temple, whether in 2 Corinthians 6 or 1 Peter 2, is faith in Jesus Christ. The contrast is between those who believe and those who do not.

The unique privilege and glory of God's temple is his presence. 'The Lord is there' (*Ezek.* 48:35). 'We are the temple of the living God; as God said, "I will make my dwelling among them and walk among them, and I will be their God, and they shall be my people"' (v. 16). This is another way of stating the truth of 1 John 1:3: 'that which we have seen and heard we proclaim also to you, so that you too may have fellowship with us; and indeed our fellowship is with the Father and with his Son Jesus Christ.' Fellowship with God is not a means to an end. It is an end in itself. We were originally made for it and, by God's grace, are now re-created in Christ for it. Fellowship with God is the new wine of the kingdom of which we are to drink daily, and will eternally.

GOD'S CALL TO HIS PEOPLE

On the basis of this understanding that God's people are his temple,

Paul issues God's call to us to be separate. 'Therefore go out from their midst, and be separate from them, says the Lord, and touch no unclean thing; then I will welcome you' (v. 17). We must recognise what this means regarding marriage, business and associations.

A distinction is to be made between our actions in those situations in which we find ourselves when we are brought to faith in Christ, and those we enter into once we have become believers. 1 Corinthians 7 makes it plain that if we are already married to a non-Christian when we are converted, we have no grounds for separation from that partner. Rather, we are to aim at winning him or her to the Lord Jesus Christ. It seems right to apply the principle to business, too. We should not do damage to non-Christian business partners by immediately cutting ourselves off from them or withdrawing from the business. That may prove to be the right course eventually, but never suddenly, without considering our Christian duty to love our neighbour as ourselves. On the other hand, it will almost certainly be right to resign immediately from organisations like the Freemasons, who with their invitation to those of all faiths and belief in human goodness, do not hold to the uniqueness of Jesus Christ and salvation through faith in him alone. This resignation will be part of our testimony to the Lord Jesus Christ.

The call to be separate is the call to be different as a result of our new relationship to God. He is holy, and his call to us is to be holy (*1 Pet.* 1:16). By holiness, more than anything else, we show we are God's children. His adopted sons and daughters want to be like him. By the achievement of such a desire, we honour God.

If he can, Satan will misrepresent holiness. He will try to obscure its attractiveness, so that we then fail to strive after it. He may encourage us to see the achievement of holiness as a ground of our acceptance with God. If he manages this, we lose sight of our dependence upon grace and fall into the folly of returning to faith in good works. If Satan cannot succeed in these misrepresentations, he may make us despair at our slow progress in holiness. He may suggest that our personal holiness is but a shadow of the reality it ought to be. True as that suggestion may be for most of us, we must remember that God's grace does not complete its work in a day. As John Newton put it, 'I am not what I ought to be, I am not what

I want to be, I am not what I hope to be in another world, but still I am not now what I once used to be, and by the grace of God I am what I am.' Robert Murray M'Cheyne's prayer is one we do well to make: 'Lord, make me as holy as a saved sinner can be.'

God calls us to enter fully into our privileges as his children. As we honestly separate ourselves from what we know displeases him, he promises, 'I will be a father to you, and you shall be sons and daughters to me, says the Lord Almighty' (v. 18). In other words, we will know the enjoyment of the present benefits of that relationship that is ours in Christ.

THE PLACE OF GOD'S PROMISES

God's promises amply encourage us to respond to his gracious call. 'Since we have these promises, beloved, let us cleanse ourselves from every defilement of body and spirit, bringing holiness to completion in the fear of God' (v. 1). His words of encouragement to us stimulate us to perform our duty.

While the enemy of souls encourages, if he can, distrust of God's promises, part of the Spirit's special work is to reveal their preciousness. His promises are the currency of our faith. We are to use them – spend them, as it were – in the support of our faith and obedience. When we pray, we are to plead his promises (*Neh.* 1:5–11). As Peter reminds us, 'His divine power has granted to us all things that pertain to life and godliness, through the knowledge of him who called us to his own glory and excellence, by which he has granted to us his precious and very great promises, so that through them you may become partakers of the divine nature, having escaped from the corruption that is in the world because of sinful desire.' (*2 Pet.* 1:3–4).

Our proper response to God's holiness and promises is to 'cleanse ourselves from every defilement of body and spirit' (v. 1). While holiness is essentially the work of the Holy Spirit, he requires our active co-operation. If our reverence for God is in place, so will be our answer to his call to holiness. When we live lives of holiness – of honest and total commitment to God – we demonstrate that we have not received God's grace in vain (*2 Cor.* 6:1)!

12

Trying to Put the Record Straight

²Make room in your hearts for us. We have wronged no one, we have corrupted no one, we have taken advantage of no one. ³I do not say this to condemn you, for I said before that you are in our hearts, to die together and to live together. ⁴I am acting with great boldness toward you; I have great pride in you; I am filled with comfort. In all our affliction, I am overflowing with joy.

⁵For even when we came into Macedonia, our bodies had no rest, but we were afflicted at every turn—fighting without and fear within. ⁶But God, who comforts the downcast, comforted us by the coming of Titus, ⁷and not only by his coming but also by the comfort with which he was comforted by you, as he told us of your longing, your mourning, your zeal for me, so that I rejoiced still more. ⁸For even if I made you grieve with my letter, I do not regret it—though I did regret it, for I see that that letter grieved you, though only for a while. ⁹As it is, I rejoice, not because you were grieved, but because you were grieved into repenting. For you felt a godly grief, so that you suffered no loss through us.

¹⁰For godly grief produces a repentance that leads to salvation without regret, whereas worldly grief produces death. ¹¹For see what earnestness this godly grief has produced in you, but also what eagerness to clear yourselves, what indignation, what fear, what longing, what zeal, what punishment! At every point you have proved yourselves innocent in the matter. ¹²So although I wrote to you, it was not for the sake of the one who did the wrong, nor for the sake of the one who suffered the wrong, but in order that your earnestness for us might be revealed to you in the sight of God. ¹³Therefore we are comforted.

And besides our own comfort, we rejoiced still more at the joy of Titus, because his spirit has been refreshed by you all. [14]For whatever boasts I made to him about you, I was not put to shame. But just as everything we said to you was true, so also our boasting before Titus has proved true. [15]And his affection for you is even greater, as he remembers the obedience of you all, how you received him with fear and trembling. [16]I rejoice, because I have perfect confidence in you (2 Cor. 7:2–16).

Paul returns again to the main reason for his letter. The Corinthians had misunderstood an earlier one, and it had cooled relationships between them. 'Make room in your hearts for us,' he urges. 'We have wronged no one, we have corrupted no one, we have taken advantage of no one' (v. 2).

Sadly, misunderstandings do happen between believers, as among all groups of people. The enemy of souls, the accuser of Christians (*Rev.* 12:10) is behind many of the upsets in the life of the church. A a nineteenth-century preacher, C. H. Spurgeon, in writing to his son, significantly urged him, 'Fight the devil and love the deacons.'

OUT INTO THE OPEN

Paul draws attention to the accusations made against him and his colleagues. News of the false charges had somehow reached him. Some Corinthians accused him and his companions of wrongdoing, corruption and exploitation (v. 2). Such complaints damaged not only their reputations but the honour of the Lord Jesus, whom they represented. If we know people are perhaps suspicious of us, or that they misunderstand our motives, it is often difficult to know what to do. One obviously good response is to persist in doing what is right, trusting that in the end the people concerned will recognise the truth about our motives. However, the situation may become so serious and unhelpful that it is better to make them aware that we know what they are saying and thinking. The devil delights in innuendoes and lies. The most effective answer to his activity sometimes is to bring things out into the open, no matter how uncomfortable that process may be.

REASSURANCES

In the face of these accusations, Paul carefully reassures the Corinthians. He and his colleagues wanted them to trust them – to make room for them in their hearts (v. 2). He assures them that the charges were without foundation. They had not wronged, corrupted or exploited anyone. The Corinthians might have interpreted such a direct answer as a rebuke. To counter this possible misinterpretation, Paul explains that he had no desire to condemn them because of the wrong things that had been said (v. 3).

The Corinthians had an established place in the hearts of Paul and his fellow workers, who wanted them to know that they were for them and ready to live or die with them (v. 3). Paul deliberately affirms his great confidence, pride, encouragement and joy in his readers. When things go wrong in relationships, one positive way to rebuild them is to affirm the good things we see in one another.

Paul indicates that the spiritual battles he had to fight had been aggravated by his worry when he had no up-to-date news of the Corinthians (vv. 5–7). However, he and his companions had been set at ease when Titus arrived with his report of his time with them and the comfort they gave him. God understands the 'fighting without' we all have at times and our 'fear within'. He knows how to relieve them, sometimes through the timely visit of a Christian friend who brings encouragement (v. 7). This was Paul's frequent experience (see, for example, *Acts* 28:15, *2 Tim.* 1:16–17). We can imagine how Paul and those with him were encouraged when Titus reported, 'The Corinthians love you. They remember you with great affection. They care about you.'

THE TRUTH ABOUT THE LETTER THAT HAD CAUSED UPSET

Paul shares the initial misgivings he had had about the letter he had sent. His feelings improved, however, as time went on, for the letter served its purpose (vv. 8–9). It upset the Corinthians to receive it, but only for a while.

Paul's letter was an exercise of pastoral discipline. Discipline is never pleasant at the time, but properly exercised and received, it produces fruit. That is why it is foolish to neglect the practice of

[79]

discipline. It is easy to shirk it because it is hard to administer if we are sensitive and caring. However, if we genuinely care for people, like parents caring for their children, we must take it on board because love demands it.

The instrument God employed to bring the Corinthians to repentance was Paul's letter: 'As it is, I rejoice, not because you were grieved, but because you were grieved into repenting. For you felt a godly grief, so that you suffered no loss through us' (v. 9). His letter – unpleasant as they found it at first – stirred them to right action. Their distress turned them to God rather than away from him. One reason we may shrink from exercising discipline is that we are afraid people will turn away from God. God sees to it, however, that properly received, spiritual discipline is all gain, with no harm!

The sorrow God uses to bring us to repentance and salvation is unlike the sorrow of the world. 'For godly grief produces a repentance that leads to salvation without regret, whereas worldly grief produces death' (v. 10). Repentance has three main ingredients: contrition, confession and conversion. It brings benefit, and never loss. 'See what earnestness this godly grief has produced in you' (v. 11). Letters plainly have pastoral use when a face to face meeting with people – always the better option – is impossible.

A PASTORAL PRINCIPLE

Paul pauses to establish an important pastoral principle. 'For see what earnestness this godly grief has produced in you, but also what eagerness to clear yourselves, what indignation, what fear, what longing, what zeal, what punishment! At every point you have proved yourselves innocent in the matter' (v. 11). Distress, whether deserved or not, may drive us to God. It then brings immeasurable gain. Such profit was great and conspicuous in the case of the Corinthians. Their godly sorrow served to prove the genuineness of their spiritual life. They became more earnest. They were eager to clear themselves. They felt greater indignation at wrong. They knew increased alarm at things that were amiss. Their longing and concern grew. They enhanced their readiness to see justice done. At every point they showed themselves eager to put things right.

THE ENCOURAGEMENT OF SPIRITUAL FRUIT

The way in which godly sorrow flowed from his appropriate exercise of pastoral discipline greatly encouraged Paul. This response was more important to him than the particular issue that first prompted his letter (v. 12). Titus' good report of his visit doubled the joy of Paul and his colleagues (v. 13). The Corinthians had welcomed him warmly and enthusiastically. Titus had been renewed and refreshed by all the Corinthians did for him. This should be the regular consequence of Christians meeting and enjoying fellowship. The good things Paul had reported to Titus about the Corinthians before his visit had proved true. Titus was impressed by their prompt obedience, and careful and sensitive hospitality (v. 15). Paul could not have been more proud of them (v. 16).

AN INVALUABLE LESSON

Paul practises a fundamental principle of good relationships. Show love to people by always seeing the best in them, whatever may be to the contrary. We are then able to try to put the record straight if that needs to be done. Difficulties are much more readily overcome if we do not aggravate them.

What Paul wrote must have helped to remove misunderstanding. We do well to ask ourselves whether we need to clear the air and put things right in any relationship.

13

Grace and Generosity

[1]We want you to know, brothers, about the grace of God that has been given among the churches of Macedonia, [2]for in a severe test of affliction, their abundance of joy and their extreme poverty have overflowed in a wealth of generosity on their part. [3]For they gave according to their means, as I can testify, and beyond their means, of their own accord, [4]begging us earnestly for the favor of taking part in the relief of the saints— [5]and this, not as we expected, but they gave themselves first to the Lord and then by the will of God to us. [6]Accordingly, we urged Titus that as he had started, so he should complete among you this act of grace. [7]But as you excel in everything—in faith, in speech, in knowledge, in all earnestness, and in our love for you—see that you excel in this act of grace also.

[8]I say this not as a command, but to prove by the earnestness of others that your love also is genuine. [9]For you know the grace of our Lord Jesus Christ, that though he was rich, yet for your sake he became poor, so that you by his poverty might become rich. [10]And in this matter I give my judgment: this benefits you, who a year ago started not only to do this work but also to desire to do it. [11]So now finish doing it as well, so that your readiness in desiring it may be matched by your completing it out of what you have. [12]For if the readiness is there, it is acceptable according to what a person has, not according to what he does not have. [13]For I do not mean that others should be eased and you burdened, but that as a matter of fairness [14]your abundance at the present time should supply their need, so that their abundance may supply your need, that there may be fairness. [15]As it is written, 'Whoever gathered much had nothing left over, and whoever gathered little had no lack' (2 Cor. 8:1–15).

Grace and Generosity

Giving is an appropriate response to grace. The one true God, who reveals himself in creation, in the Scriptures and in his Son, is 'the giving God' (*James* 1:5). Nowhere is that seen more wonderfully than in his gift of his Son to be our Saviour, the atoning sacrifice for our sins (*John* 3:16, *1 John* 4:10). Paul refers to this unspeakable love gift here (v. 9) and later (9:15). It is the foundation of all he now writes about giving and generosity in giving.

When we receive the grace of the Lord Jesus in salvation, grace gets to work in us making us more like our heavenly Father. That inevitably means we become more like him in generous giving. Generosity is a Christian grace. That is not to imply that people who are not Christians are ungenerous. Many put us to shame by their unselfishness. All Christians, however, are marked by increasing generosity as they grow in the grace and knowledge of our Lord Jesus Christ.

As we noticed earlier, the proper response to grace is gratitude, and where gratitude exists there is invariably joy – the joy of thankfulness and appreciation. The joy God gives us in his Son is an 'abundance of joy', and it wells up 'in a wealth of generosity' as we become aware of the needs of others (v. 2). Since such joy is not inhibited by poverty, so its generosity is not limited. Christian joy prompts us to give as much as we are able, and even beyond our ability (v. 3; cf. *Mark* 12:41–44). It should not need to be prompted by others (v. 3).

Giving is an essential ingredient of Christian service. By giving we are able to help fellow Christians – 'the saints' – who are in need, whether close at hand or abroad (v. 4), as well as those whose needs are brought before us (*Gal.* 6:10). It is a privilege to give, since in giving to them we express thankfulness to the Lord himself.

There is an unexpected element in Christian giving (v. 5). As we receive fresh glimpses of God's goodness to us in his Son, our joy prompts renewed devotion to the Lord Jesus. We first give ourselves to him and then to others, according to God's will. Along with the giving of ourselves goes the will to be generous. The extent of our commitment to the Lord Jesus Christ may be difficult to evaluate. Nevertheless, our cheque stubs say something significant. Commitment to the Lord Jesus Christ leads us to go beyond what any might expect us to do (v. 5).

[83]

THE EXAMPLE OF THE MACEDONIAN CHURCHES

The Macedonian churches excelled in expressions of gratitude to God. They underwent severe trial (v. 2), but they discovered – as all Christians do – that God gives grace to us in our trials. If we did not meet with trials and difficulties, we might never learn to appreciate the joy God's grace and help bring. The Macedonian Christians' joy then overflowed in generous giving as the poverty of others was brought to their notice. Although needy themselves, they counted it a privilege to share what they possessed with Christians who had even less (v. 4). They did not limit their giving to putting money into the offering plate. They put themselves in with the offering (v. 5)!

TITUS' RESPONSIBILITY

Titus' responsibility was to complete the arrangements for the same relief offering from the Corinthians (v. 6). He had evidently begun this task earlier. Now he was to see it through to completion. Paul returns to say more about Titus' task later in the chapter.

THE CHALLENGE TO THE CORINTHIANS

Paul presents to the Corinthians the challenge of the Macedonians' example (vv. 7–8). Comparisons are sometimes dangerous, especially when we foolishly compare ourselves with others out of motives of pride. If, however, we test ourselves by the good example of others, the exercise becomes beneficial.

When the Corinthians' faith, speech, knowledge, earnestness and love were examined, they received top marks. However, the reality of these graces or virtues required the confirmation of practical generosity. Faith without works is dead. Faith in the Lord Jesus produces generosity. It is not enough to talk about generosity; speech must issue in deeds. Knowledge of God produces likeness to God – the giving God. Genuine concern for others means we strive to meet people's needs, as love does.

Paul did not want to command the Corinthians to give. Rather, as they heard of the Macedonians' example, he wanted them to test the sincerity of their profession of love for the Lord Jesus and his people. None of them would have doubted the rightness of the

Macedonians' giving, prompted it as it was by the grace of the Lord Jesus (v. 9). His grace is the supreme example to follow. Paul reminds them, 'Though he was rich, yet for your sake he became poor, so that you by his poverty might become rich'. If the Corinthians' love was sincere, the Macedonians' example would stimulate them to follow their Lord's example.

PAUL'S ADVICE

Paul's advice was that the Corinthians should finish with enthusiasm what they had begun (vv. 10–15). When Titus began his work among them, they had made promises or resolutions to give. Now it was time for them to fulfil their commitment. What we purpose and promise to give, we should complete.

When the time for keeping promises arrives, our circumstances have sometimes changed and we cannot do as much as we originally hoped. While we must deeply regret any inability to give what we intended or promised, the desire to give is as vital as the giving itself (v. 10). Our willingness is important to God, and that makes our gifts acceptable to him, whatever they are (v. 12).

Behind all Christian giving is God's intention that a measure of material equality should be achieved among Christians (vv. 13–14). As we give, our plenty supplies the needs of others. Although now may be the occasion for us to give to them, there may come a moment when they give to us. There is a time for giving, and a time for receiving. Spiritual principles operate when we give. Paul quotes one from the book of Exodus, 'Whoever gathered much had nothing left over, and whoever gathered little had no lack' (v. 15; *Exod.* 16:18).

14

The Purpose of the Visit to Corinth of Titus and His Companions

[16]*But thanks be to God, who put into the heart of Titus the same earnest care I have for you.* [17]*For he not only accepted our appeal, but being himself very earnest he is going to you of his own accord.* [18]*With him we are sending the brother who is famous among all the churches for his preaching of the gospel.* [19]*And not only that, but he has been appointed by the churches to travel with us as we carry out this act of grace that is being ministered by us, for the glory of the Lord himself and to show our good will.* [20]*We take this course so that no one should blame us about this generous gift that is being administered by us,* [21]*for we aim at what is honorable not only in the Lord's sight but also in the sight of man.* [22]*And with them we are sending our brother whom we have often tested and found earnest in many matters, but who is now more earnest than ever because of his great confidence in you.* [23]*As for Titus, he is my partner and fellow worker for your benefit. And as for our brothers, they are messengers of the churches, the glory of Christ.* [24]*So give proof before the churches of your love and of our boasting about you to these men.*

[1]*Now it is superfluous for me to write to you about the ministry for the saints,* [2]*for I know your readiness, of which I boast about you to the people of Macedonia, saying that Achaia has been ready since last year. And your zeal has stirred up most of them.* [3]*But I am sending the brothers so that our boasting about you may not prove empty in this matter, so that you may be ready, as I said you would be.* [4]*Otherwise, if some Macedonians come with me and find that you are not ready, we would be humiliated—to say nothing of you—for being so*

confident. ⁵So I thought it necessary to urge the brothers to go on ahead to you and arrange in advance for the gift you have promised, so that it may be ready as a willing gift, not as an exaction (2 Cor. 8:16–9:5).

Paul has mentioned Titus already in verse 6 as the person commissioned to set in motion the Corinthians' giving for the relief of 'the poor among the saints at Jerusalem' (*Rom.* 15:26). Titus was a Greek (*Gal.* 2:3), and Paul's 'true' son in the faith (*Titus* 1:4), in that he had been brought to faith through Paul. He was of exemplary character. He did not serve for any personal advantage, and he never sought to exploit people (*2 Cor.* 12:18). He had become one of Paul's regular companions – a 'partner and fellow worker' (v. 23). Paul now expresses his thanksgiving to God for Titus, and in particular for his sharing of Paul's concern for the Corinthians (v. 16). When asked to visit them, Titus had not simply said yes, but he had responded enthusiastically. He would have wanted to do so whether asked or not (v. 17).

Paul links with Titus an unnamed Christian who would accompany him (vv. 18–19). His presence underlined the importance of the task, because he was a person 'famous among all the churches for his preaching of the gospel'. Furthermore, he had been 'appointed by the churches' to accompany Paul and his colleagues as they carried out their responsibility of conveying the gift to its intended recipients. The word 'appointed' indicates that the churches had undertaken their selection seriously, with perhaps the churches voting upon their choice.

It would be interesting to know the identity of this 'brother', and we may wonder why Paul does not give his name. However, it reminds us that many unnamed Christians do sterling work in the interests of Christ's kingdom. Although their identity is unknown to us, it is not to God. Better by far to be known by him than by our fellow men and women.

THE PURPOSE OF THE COLLECTION AND OFFERING

The word 'offering' is preferable to 'collection' when referring to what we give to God. Paul describes it here as an 'act of grace', reminding us that all our giving to God is a response to, and a proof of, his grace (v. 19). However, when any offering is made, it has to be collected and administered! That was the task of Paul, Titus and others.

The intention was that the collection should be a spiritual sacrifice (cf. *Heb.* 13:16). Genuine giving to God is an 'act of grace' (v. 19). It is given not so much in response to a command but as an expression of grateful love to the Lord. While it has in view the meeting of other people's needs, our eyes are primarily upon the sacrifice of the Lord Jesus and the example of his generous self-giving (v. 9).

The purpose of the offering was for the glory of the Lord himself (v. 19). There were several ways in which the offering might show their respect for him. Its largeness would have expressed the gratitude they felt for the grace of the Lord Jesus. Its spontaneity would have signified the joy they found in knowing God through his Son. Its costliness would have exhibited to unbelievers the sacrificial love of God, whose example they imitated.

The purpose of the offering was to show Christian good will towards brothers and sisters in need (v. 19). Tangible expressions of love mean much when we pass through difficult times. Christians in Jerusalem were going to be encouraged not only by the gifts they received but by the love and concern they represented.

THE CARE REQUIRED IN HANDLING MONEY

Paul felt the heavy responsibility of administering the gifts of God's people. The liberality of their giving only increased this sense of accountability (v. 20). People differ in their carefulness about money, whether their own or that of others. Some never borrow from others, and some never lend, but rather give. Some are careless in keeping records, whereas others are meticulous, whether in dealing with small or large sums of money. Disparities in people's dispositions and habits make all the more necessary the careful and conscientious administration of any money placed in our care.

The scrupulous management of money in the church is essential. If gifts are to honour the Lord, there must not be the slightest impropriety. Three principles in this passage guide us. First, we are to avoid blame over the way in which we administer the money God's people give (v. 20). There should be no grounds for people finding fault with our stewardship. Second, we are to aim at what is honourable, not only in God's sight but also in the eyes of our fellow men and women (v. 21). Third, by implication, it is better if responsibility for the care of money is shared, rather than left to one person (vv. 18–22).

THOSE WHO HONOUR CHRIST ARE TO BE HONOURED

Paul mentions another unnamed 'brother' who accompanied Titus and the earlier anonymous Christian (v. 22). He too had been well proved for his spiritual zeal. So far as the Corinthians were concerned, he was an ideal choice because he had 'great confidence' in them. All three were not only 'messengers of the churches' but 'the glory of Christ' (v. 23). No higher tribute could have been given. Their lives spoke well of their Master and made them 'adorn the doctrine of our God and Saviour' (*Titus* 2:10).

Such representatives of the churches deserved to be honoured by all the Corinthians as they went about their task. God's people at Corinth were able to demonstrate their love by generous hospitality and practical help to aid them in the completion of their work. They were able to honour them by Christlike behaviour and helpfulness that justified the pride of the apostle and his colleagues in them (v. 24). They were able to honour them by treating them so well that wherever they went among the churches they carried a good report of the Corinthians.

AN IMPORTANT REASON FOR THE VISIT OF THE REPRESENTATIVES OF THE CHURCHES (9:1–5)

It was the task of Titus and his two companions to guarantee the Corinthians' readiness to complete their promised giving (v. 4). Paul had no doubts about their eagerness to help and had boasted to the Macedonians about it (v. 2). He had even used the Corinthians' zeal to stir them to action (v. 2)! However, he was not so sure about their state of readiness to do what they had promised. Aware that when he arrived, he might have Macedonians with him, he did not want either himself or the Corinthians to be ashamed at any unreadiness to give, or perhaps to give unwillingly, because they had not anticipated it being required so soon (v. 5).

Paul repeats five truths about giving. First, it is 'ministry for the saints' (v. 1). Second, the example of others may stir us to give more generously (v. 2). Third, our giving requires careful administration by others to make sure it reaches its proper destinations (vv. 3–5). Fourth, it is good to make considered promises to God – and sometimes to others – about what we intend to give (v. 5). Fifth, our giving is to be eager, enthusiastic and cheerful, the opposite of a grudging attitude or unwillingness to give (vv. 2,5).

15

Giving: Principles to Remember and Blessings Promised

⁶The point is this: whoever sows sparingly will also reap sparingly, and whoever sows bountifully will also reap bountifully. ⁷Each one must give as he has decided in his heart, not reluctantly or under compulsion, for God loves a cheerful giver. ⁸And God is able to make all grace abound to you, so that having all sufficiency in all things at all times, you may abound in every good work. ⁹As it is written,

> *'He has distributed freely, he has given to the poor;*
> *his righteousness endures forever.'*

¹⁰He who supplies seed to the sower and bread for food will supply and multiply your seed for sowing and increase the harvest of your righteousness. ¹¹You will be enriched in every way to be generous in every way, which through us will produce thanksgiving to God. ¹²For the ministry of this service is not only supplying the needs of the saints but is also overflowing in many thanksgivings to God. ¹³By their approval of this service, they will glorify God because of your submission flowing from your confession of the gospel of Christ, and the generosity of your contribution for them and for all others, ¹⁴while they long for you and pray for you, because of the surpassing grace of God upon you. ¹⁵Thanks be to God for his inexpressible gift!
(2 Cor. 9:6–15)

Teaching about giving is found throughout the Bible, in both the Old and New Testaments. This section of Paul's second letter is particularly pointed in establishing principles that are to govern Christian giving.

GIVING IS SOWING

In verse 6 Paul quotes a saying probably familiar to first-century Christians: 'Whoever sows sparingly will also reap sparingly, and whoever sows bountifully will also reap bountifully.' It is a dictum to be remembered. Generous giving brings its own reward. The verse matches Proverbs 11:24–25: 'One gives freely, yet grows all the richer; another withholds what he should give, and only suffers want.' Proverbs 22:9 speaks of the great reward of God's blessing: 'Whoever has a bountiful eye will be blessed, for he shares his bread with the poor.' Our Lord Jesus taught, 'give, and it will be given to you. Good measure, pressed down, shaken together, running over, will be put into your lap. For with the measure you use it will be measured back to you' (*Luke* 6:38). The illustration Paul uses of harvest is striking. Thin sowing leads to thin reaping. Giving is as sensible an exercise as a farmer sowing for a harvest.

GIVING IS PERSONAL

Nowhere does Paul suggest that the possession of wealth is sin. Material prosperity does bring the responsibility, however, of using it wisely. Yet the way in which we disburse our gifts is a private and individual matter (v. 7). We need to think about it seriously and make our own decisions. Both the purpose behind the gifts and the choice of recipients are our own. Sometimes groups of Christians have been authoritarian in dictating the proportion of their income that Christians should give. The motivation behind this may not always have been the highest, and it is not justified.

Our individual circumstances vary, including the demands that family and others legitimately make upon our personal earnings. When we seek God's wisdom to use our money and resources well, right convictions soon emerge as to how we should carry out our responsibilities. I am responsible for my own income. I am not responsible for other people's stewardship.

GIVING IS TO BE CHEERFUL

Whatever decisions we arrive at about our giving, they should be happy ones. If they are reluctant or made under a sense of compulsion, they will not be glad. 'God loves a cheerful giver'

(v. 7). The Lord Jesus taught that a widow's 'two small copper coins' had greater potential to please God than the giving of rich people, though their giving exceeded the widow's many times over (*Luke* 21:1– 4). When we visit a home that has young children, it is always a pleasure when a child spontaneously offers us a sweet, even if we do not enjoy them. We find little pleasure in such an offer when a parent cajoles or commands it! Our heavenly Father delights not only in what we give but even more in how we give.

GIVING IS REWARDED BY GOD

Paul returns to the picture of sowing and harvesting. He quotes Psalm 112:9, which describes the happiness of the individual who fears God and gives generously (v. 9). Generous giving and practical righteousness are indissolubly linked: 'he has distributed freely, he has given to the poor; his righteousness endures for ever.'

Twin thoughts about harvest find expression here. First, God looks for a harvest of righteousness because of his own good work in us. One of the fruits of his Spirit's activity in us is generosity. Essential to the harvest of righteousness from our lives is delight in giving (v. 10). Second, as we love to give, God rewards it by his super-abounding grace. We then find we have all we require to continue to 'abound in every good work' (v. 8).

One of the amazing truths about giving – sometimes too intimate and personal to talk about – is that we never give generously without discovering afresh God's ability to supply our personal needs. Generous giving may appear hazardous when we do not possess very much, but it is not so when we recognise God's ability (v. 8). Our heavenly Father is the universal provider (*Isa.* 55:10), who is well able to supply his children's requirements!

GIVING INCREASES OUR ABILITY TO GIVE

We have more than hinted at this profound truth already. When we give, God may often graciously choose to supply and multiply our resources, to increase the harvest of our righteousness (v. 10). Part of God's purpose in making lavish provision for us is so that we may provide liberally for others (v. 8). God never allows us to be in his debt. As we are generous, he enriches us in every way.

He makes us rich to make it possible for us to be always generous (v. 11)!

This principle must not be misunderstood or wrongly applied. We must not, and do not, give to God and his work with this as our motivation. There must be no 'penny in the slot' mentality about our giving. The way God enriches us may not always be financial, since financial blessings are not the most important. Nevertheless, all who give generously and cheerfully know something of the 'miracle' and 'surprise' of God's returning and recurring provision.

GIVING SUPPLIES THE NEEDS OF GOD'S PEOPLE

God has no need of our money. All the resources of heaven and earth are his! He has chosen, however, that by the generous giving of his church, the needs of all his people may be met (v. 12). In chapter 8 Paul establishes the principle that the primary purpose of our giving to God is service to the saints (v. 4).

God supplies the material and financial necessities of all his people. His foremost provision for most of us is by means of daily work and the health to pursue it. For others, however, daily work that brings remuneration is not possible, either because of unemployment or ill health, or perhaps because they are engaged all their time in the service of the gospel. Then God places upon the heart of those with greater resources the need of those who do not have as much. From time to time we find the names, faces and situations of people coming to mind, and often in a way that suggests they require encouragement and financial support. We are wise not to push such thoughts aside, but rather to ponder them and, more often than not, determine to act.

GIVING RESULTS IN THANKSGIVING TO GOD

Our chief end is to glorify God. This summing up in the Shorter Catechism of our purpose in life expresses the teaching of the whole Bible. Those who benefit from the timely and ample giving of God's people unfailingly give God praise. It is he who prompted the giving and enabled the givers to give. He has shown the givers that generous giving is part of the obedience that accompanies their 'confession of the gospel of Christ' (v. 13).

As a pastor, I have often had the privilege of delivering anonymous gifts from God's people to the intended recipients. I have come to recognise that it is not always easy to be on the receiving end of the generosity of others. However, when we recognise God's hand in it, we cannot but acknowledge his unfailing love and goodness. The joy, gratitude and thanksgiving to God that follow are undoubtedly a spiritual sacrifice to him. That the gifts have been anonymous has directed the thanksgiving all the more clearly to him.

Here is a wonderful motive for giving: people overflow into 'many thanksgivings to God' (v. 12)! They praise him not only for the gift, but also for the mutual sharing that is fundamental to the well-being of the body of Christ (v. 13).

THE RIGHT PLACE TO END

Early in his discussion of Christian giving, Paul points to the grace of the Lord Jesus who became poor that we might become rich (*2 Cor.* 8:9). Significantly, it is where he also ends: 'Thanks be to God for his inexpressible gift!' (v. 15)

In all our giving, from beginning to end, our eyes must be on our Saviour and God's indescribable kindness in giving him to us. Christian giving, properly understood, is our response to that gift. When our eyes are on our Saviour, giving is never a problem!

16

Paul's Defence of His Ministry

¹I, Paul, myself entreat you, by the meekness and gentleness of Christ—I who am humble when face to face with you, but bold toward you when I am away!— ²I beg of you that when I am present I may not have to show boldness with such confidence as I count on showing against some who suspect us of walking according to the flesh. ³For though we walk in the flesh, we are not waging war according to the flesh. ⁴For the weapons of our warfare are not of the flesh but have divine power to destroy strongholds. ⁵We destroy arguments and every lofty opinion raised against the knowledge of God, and take every thought captive to obey Christ, ⁶being ready to punish every disobedience, when your obedience is complete.

⁷Look at what is before your eyes. If anyone is confident that he is Christ's, let him remind himself that just as he is Christ's, so also are we. ⁸For even if I boast a little too much of our authority, which the Lord gave for building you up and not for destroying you, I will not be ashamed. ⁹I do not want to appear to be frightening you with my letters. ¹⁰For they say, 'His letters are weighty and strong, but his bodily presence is weak, and his speech of no account.' ¹¹Let such a person understand that what we say by letter when absent, we do when present. ¹²Not that we dare to classify or compare ourselves with some of those who are commending themselves. But when they measure themselves by one another and compare themselves with one another, they are without understanding.

¹³But we will not boast beyond limits, but will boast only with regard to the area of influence God assigned to us, to reach even to you. ¹⁴For we are not overextending ourselves, *as though we did not reach you. For we were the first to come all the way to you with the gospel of Christ. ¹⁵We do not boast beyond limit in the labours of others. But our hope is that as your faith increases, our area of influence among you may be greatly enlarged, ¹⁶so that we may preach the gospel in lands beyond you, without boasting of work already done in another's area of influence. ¹⁷'Let the one who boasts, boast in the Lord.' ¹⁸For it is not the one who commends himself who is approved, but the one whom the Lord commends* (2 Cor. 10:1–18).

Throughout this letter we sense Paul's concern about the criticisms and false accusations made against him by some at Corinth. The perpetrators were probably individuals who had attached themselves to religious teachers who opposed the apostle's contribution and influence in the church. It must have been a problem to Paul to know to what extent he should try to answer the fault-finders and critics. There is a time to be silent (*Eccles.* 3:7; cf. *Matt.* 27:14). This is especially the case when we realise that the most God-honouring thing to do usually is not to stand up for ourselves but to leave our vindication to God (cf. *1 Pet.* 2:23).

No doubt the reason for Paul's attempt to answer some of the allegations and smears against his character was his God-given relationship to many of the Corinthians. He was their spiritual father (*1 Cor.* 4:15). If people's confidence in his character was undermined, then their faith in God's truth, which he had declared to them, was also under threat (*i.e. 1 Cor.* 15:1–8). The enemy of souls is skilled in his evil work. To recognise Paul's dilemma increases our sympathy and understanding of what he writes.

SEEDS OF DOUBT

We may identify four unhelpful seeds of doubt that had been sown in the minds of the Corinthians concerning Paul's character. Four accusations had been levelled against him. *The first accusation was that he was guilty of cowardice.* He was accused of being 'humble' when face to face with the Corinthians but 'bold' when away from them (v. 1). He was charged with being timid when with them, but a bully when absent.

The second accusation was that he was worldly and lacking in spirituality. Some suggested that his behaviour was governed by the standards of the world, 'according to the flesh' (v. 2). This was equivalent to accusing him of deviousness.

The third suggestion was that Paul and his colleagues were suspect members of the church. It seems to have been suggested that they did not genuinely belong to Christ (v. 7). Doubts were cast upon their regeneration.

When we do not agree with the position people take upon some issue, it is all too easy to imagine or even suggest that perhaps they are not true Christians. If our judgment is false, how much we must grieve the Holy Spirit who has brought them to the same new birth as ourselves.

The fourth suggestion was that Paul and those who worked with him were second-class servants of the Lord Jesus. They were compared with others and ranked in order of importance or ability (v. 12). We sense something of this attitude from his first letter (see *1 Cor.* 1:12). Once we attach ourselves to individual teachers or leaders rather than to the Lord Jesus himself, we soon begin putting them into league tables, and valuing some more than others. All four suggestions came from the same source – the evil one.

A DEFENCE

Paul answers each accusation and suggestion. He does so for the reason we suggested earlier. His relationship as spiritual father to many of the Corinthians meant that undermining his position could ultimately undermine their faith. Our purpose is to look now at the accusations one by one and consider his answers.

COWARDICE

The answer to this suggestion is not detailed. While it was appropriate that Paul should answer the accusation, he did not appeal to the Corinthians on the basis of his God-given authority as an apostle, but rather 'by the meekness and gentleness of Christ' (v. 1). He wanted to plead with them as he knew the Lord himself would do – with meekness and gentleness, two aspects of the Spirit's fruit in every Christian's life (*Gal.* 5:22–23).

[98]

Meekness is an essential aspect of Christian character. Its practice means we will not quickly take offence. Some small injustice, unkind word or action will not immediately upset us, making us cause a fuss. At the same time, we will avoid at all costs needlessly upsetting others by thoughtlessness and insensitivity. Matthew Henry puts it well when writing on Matthew 5:5:

> The meek are those who quietly submit themselves to God, to his Word and to his rod, who follow his directions, and comply with his designs, and are gentle towards all men (Titus 3:2), who can hear provocation without being inflamed by it; are either silent, or return a soft answer; and who can show their displeasure, where there is occasion for it, without being transported into any indecencies; who can be cold when others are hot; and in their patience keep possession of their own souls, when they can scarcely keep possession of anything else. They are the meek, who are rarely and hardly provoked, but quickly and easily pacified; and who would rather forgive twenty injuries than revenge one, having the rule of their own spirits.

Along with meekness goes gentleness (v. 1). When Isaiah prophesied about the Messiah, he declared that the Servant of the Lord 'He will not cry aloud or lift up his voice, or make it heard in the street; a bruised reed he will not break, and a faintly burning wick he will not quench' (*Isa.* 42:2–3). While always pursuing truth and righteousness, our Lord Jesus was never loud, aggressive or threatening, even when wrongly accused or maligned. Meekness and gentleness char-acterised his earthly life and ministry. As we grow in our knowledge of him, these characteristics will similarly mark us. They are essential in any pastoral care we exercise.

Paul exhibits meekness and gentleness in the language he employs. Notice his use of the word 'beg' (v. 2). He begged the Corinthians that they would make it unnecessary for him to prove them wrong when eventually he revisited them.

The accusation of verse 1 is repeated in another form in verse 10, and it makes sense to consider the two verses together. 'For they say, "his letters are weighty and strong, but his bodily presence is weak, and his speech is of no account."'

Here Paul's critics suggested that there was no substance to his letters, and that he would never do what he said he would. It is not dissimilar from the accusation referred to in chapter one, where some had said this about his promises (v. 17). It seems sensible to assume that the people who made these unhelpful and uncharitable suggestions had not been in Corinth when Paul first established the church there. He simply states that when he and his colleagues do arrive in Corinth, their critics will soon see that what they are in their letters they are when present

WORLDLY AND UNSPIRITUAL

The second accusation was of worldliness and lack of spirituality. Paul tackles this allegation head on: 'For though we walk in the flesh, we are not waging war according to the flesh' (v. 3). Paul, like us, had to live in the world. That is essential to God's present purpose for his people, his church. Living in the world, however, Paul and his colleagues did not wage war as the world does. He immediately puts this accusation in the context of the spiritual battle in which all Christians are engaged.

There are two dangers regarding spiritual conflict: either totally to neglect its reality or to go overboard and focus too much upon it. Satan delights in our going to either extreme. To encourage us in lack of balance is one of his principal and most subtle temptations.

Paul recognised the difference between the manner in which the world engages in war, and the way in which Christians are to wage war in the spiritual realm. The world conducts war with human and material weapons. It practises political manoeuvring and deviousness. Paul has already written against such tactics on the part of Christians in chapter 4 (v. 2).

As Christian believers, our proper weapons are God-given and spiritual rather than human and material. Paul indicates this in the passage from which we have just quoted, for it continues and points out a contrast in our approach to that of the world. Having said, 'We refuse to practice cunning or to tamper with God's word', he continues, 'but by the open statement of the truth we would commend ourselves to everyone's conscience in the sight of God' (4:2). This weapon of truth and other spiritual weapons are identified in Ephesians 6:10–18. Our union with the Lord Jesus, the careful practice of truth and righteousness, the straightforward declaration of the gospel, the daily experience of salvation, and the active use of the Scriptures and prayer are powerful spiritual hardware. They have 'divine power to destroy strongholds' (v. 4).

The 'strongholds' (v. 4), whatever visible or subtle form they take, are Satan's. He aids and abets men and women in arguments and pretensions that oppose the true knowledge of God. He encourages deceptive fantasies, proud arguments and barriers of human pride. In particular, he prompts people to deny the authority of our Lord Jesus Christ. We, however, know our Lord Jesus to be the head over every power and to possess unique authority (*Col.* 2:10). In his name, with our God-given weapons, we may demolish Satan's 'strongholds' (v. 4). We may knock them down like skittles. We can make rebels captives of the Lord Jesus – the happy captives of his love and grace. Paul himself was an outstanding example of a rebel turned disciple of the Lord Jesus. Those who deny our Lord Jesus' authority may be transformed into people whose one desire is to obey him!

SUSPECT MEMBERS OF THE BODY OF CHRIST

The third insinuation of the critics of Paul and his colleagues was that they were suspect members of the visible body of Christ. The basis of the accusation appears to have been his confidence about his authority as an apostle in relation to the Corinthians (v. 8).

To be viewed as suspect members of the body of Christ is a particularly sad and damaging suggestion to handle. Those who engaged in such a whispering campaign were judging by the wrong criteria (v. 7). Those who presumed to make such a judgment displayed dangerous self-confidence about their position and standing.

Paul might well have chosen to express his thoughts and perhaps doubts about his critics' relationship to Christ. Rather, however, than responding in kind, he urges everyone involved to look at obvious facts. When others take a different and sometimes opposite view to ourselves, we should not immediately question their relationship to the Lord Jesus. Unfortunately, that does happen! It occurs sometimes, for example, when Christians discuss subjects like election, baptism, the gifts of the Spirit and church government.

The basic evidence or proof of belonging to the Lord Jesus is found in 2 Timothy 2:19: 'But God's firm foundation stands, bearing this seal: "The Lord knows those who are his," and, "Let everyone who names the name of the Lord depart from iniquity."'

Paul received his authority to be an apostle from the Lord Jesus. For him not to have exercised his calling would have been a denial of his Lord. Nevertheless he is careful to explain and stress the nature of this authority. It was for the building up of God's people rather than their destruction (v. 8). This explains in part why he exhorted and appealed to them 'by the meekness and gentleness of Christ' (v. 1).

Paul was not ashamed of his mandate to build up God's people (v. 8). Rather, he boasted of it with an appropriate kind of boasting. For this reason he neither wanted nor intended to frighten the Corinthians (v. 9). His letters were, however, a necessary exercise of his apostolic and pastoral commission.

SECOND-CLASS SERVANTS OF CHRIST

The fourth suggestion of the critics of Paul and his companions was that they were second-class servants of Christ. It would seem that these detractors were not slow to tell the Corinthians how much better and superior they themselves were (v. 12). It is one thing to write our CV, but another to write our own references! Paul's critics did not hesitate to do both!

Paul's detractors were suggesting, in effect, that there are rankings among Christians. We are not immune from this snare. By the manner in which we talk or act, we may imply that certain local churches are first class whereas others are not. We may regard particular preachers as in the first rank and others as inferior. Before we know what we are doing, we act as judges. However, God alone is able to judge both churches and individuals and to evaluate the true worth of their work. We should beware of this snare, since it leads us to think as the world thinks. It is presumption on our part. Hence Paul writes, 'Not that we dare' (v. 12). To measure or compare ourselves with others is always unwise.

Paul admits the limits of even proper boasting. 'For even if I boast a little too much of our authority, which the Lord gave for building you up and not for destroying you, I will not be ashamed' (v. 8). 'But we will not boast beyond limits, but will boast only with regard to the area of influence God assigned to us, to reach even to you' (v. 13). The only judgment we may really give about our own work and service is in terms of any sphere or task to which God has plainly called us. The apostle knew that there was no uncertainty about the Lord's call to him to preach the gospel to the Corinthians (v. 13, *Acts* 18:9–10).

Paul was particularly careful to ensure that his evangelism and missionary enterprise were genuinely pioneer work (*Rom.* 15:20). When he arrived in Corinth, his purpose was to see a church established there. The Lord Jesus appeared to him in a vision assuring him that he was in the right place. Any pride in what the Lord had accomplished in Corinth, therefore, was entirely appropriate.

In boasting about their special relationship to the Corinthians, Paul and his fellow workers were not taking credit away from others (v. 15). Their hope was that God's work in and through the Corinthians would continue and thus enlarge their sphere of activity as they worked from Corinth to surrounding areas (v. 16). Paul hastens to draw attention to the danger of human boasting (v. 17). This is an Old Testament principle (*Jer.* 9:23-24), and one with which Paul's first readers were well acquainted from his earlier letter (*1 Cor.* 1:31). All pride and boasting are put in their place: 'For it is not the one who commends himself who is approved, but the one whom the Lord commends' (v. 18). Paul did not enjoy having to defend himself against these harmful accusations and insinuations. However, we have cause to be grateful that out of it emerges again this all-important truth: 'Let the one who boasts boast in the Lord.'

17

Honest Talk about Dangers

¹I wish you would bear with me in a little foolishness. Do bear with me! ²For I feel a divine jealousy for you, since I betrothed you to one husband, to present you as a pure virgin to Christ. ³But I am afraid that as the serpent deceived Eve by his cunning, your thoughts will be led astray from a sincere and pure devotion to Christ. ⁴For if someone comes and proclaims another Jesus than the one we proclaimed, or if you receive a different spirit from the one you received, or if you accept a different gospel from the one you accepted, you put up with it readily enough. ⁵Indeed, I consider that I am not in the least inferior to these super-apostles. ⁶Even if I am unskilled in speaking, I am not so in knowledge; indeed, in every way we have made this plain to you in all things.

⁷Or did I commit a sin in humbling myself so that you might be exalted, because I preached God's gospel to you free of charge? ⁸I robbed other churches by accepting support from them in order to serve you. ⁹And when I was with you and was in need, I did not burden anyone, for the brothers who came from Macedonia supplied my need. So I refrained and will refrain from burdening you in any way. ¹⁰As the truth of Christ is in me, this boasting of mine will not be silenced in the regions of Achaia. ¹¹And why? Because I do not love you? God knows I do!

¹²And what I do I will continue to do, in order to undermine the claim of those who would like to claim that in their boasted mission they work on the same terms as we do. ¹³For such men are false apostles, deceitful workmen, disguising themselves as apostles of Christ. ¹⁴And no wonder, for even Satan disguises himself as an angel of light. [15]So it is no surprise if his servants, also, disguise themselves as servants of righteousness. Their end will correspond to their deeds (2 Cor. 11:1–15).

The various writers of the books of the Bible did not write them in chapters and verses. Each book has been divided that way for ease of reference. Inevitably chapter divisions are sometimes artificial. That is the case here in 2 Corinthians where Paul's discussion of issues spans several chapters, and where he returns often to the same theme.

Paul felt compelled to write honestly about those who opposed him at Corinth and who had poisoned minds against him. Their opposition to an apostle was serious, since the Lord Jesus said, 'Whoever receives you receives me, and whoever receives me receives the one who sent me' (*Matt.* 10:40). Paul does not raise the sensitive issue of his apostolic authority for his own sake. He has just written, 'For it is not the one who commends himself who is approved, but the one whom the Lord commends' (10:18). In refusing to receive Paul, his opponents were refusing to accept the one who sent him.

DANGERS PAUL SENSED

1. Deception
Paul feared that the Corinthians were being misled. 'But I am afraid that as the serpent deceived Eve by his cunning, your thoughts will be led astray from a sincere and pure devotion to Christ' (v. 3). Satan is skilled in deception. In the case of Eve, he made her question what God had said and to doubt God's motive behind the prohibition against eating from the tree in the middle of the garden (*Gen.* 3:1–7). He deliberately encouraged her to question God's integrity.

When Satan raises up false teachers and other opponents of God's servants, he makes them sound plausible by their fine-sounding arguments.

2. Wandering from Christ
Paul sensed that through Satan's deceptive activity, the Corinthians were in danger of wandering from Christ. 'I am afraid that . . . your thoughts will be led astray from a sincere and pure devotion to Christ'

(v. 3). Significantly, the main way in which Paul feared this might happen was by someone coming to them and preaching a Jesus other than the Jesus whom he and his associates had preached (v. 4).

This danger is always present, and in subtle ways. When people propagate ideas for which they want religious or Christian support, they may sometimes try to suggest that they obtain their views from Jesus and his teaching. This tendency shows itself in all sorts of emphases, thoughts and notions. In recent decades, for example, political groups among deprived people have proclaimed Jesus as the great Liberator. Of course, as our Saviour he is the one who leads us to freedom. However, to proclaim him supremely as a political Saviour is to distort the truth about him and to end up preaching another Jesus. By such emphases people are led away from the true knowledge of Jesus and the new way of life that flows from it.

3. A different spirit

Paul refers to the possibility of the Corinthians receiving 'a different spirit from the one you received' (v. 4). A marvellous benefit of God-given faith in the Lord Jesus is the gift of the Holy Spirit. We receive the Spirit of sonship, and by him we cry, 'Abba, Father.' 'The Spirit himself bears witness with our spirit that we are children of God' (*Rom.* 8:16).

The Holy Spirit always focuses our attention upon our Lord Jesus Christ and what he has done for us. He intends us to give the Lord Jesus the pre-eminence and supremacy in everything. He wants us to maintain right views and understanding of our Saviour.

If our attention wanders from the Lord Jesus, or we begin to foster false ideas about his work and teaching, then that distraction comes from another spirit, a spirit doing the work of Satan.

4. A different gospel

When Paul first visited Corinth and preached the gospel there, he passed on to them as of first importance that 'Christ died for our sins in accordance with the Scriptures, that he was buried, that he was raised on the third day in accordance with the Scriptures, and that he appeared to Cephas, then to the twelve' (*1 Cor.* 15:3–5). He taught much more than this, but these were the crucial truths the Corinthians received, and on which they took their stand and were saved (*1 Cor.* 15:1–2).

The gospel of the glory and grace of God is the church's treasure. Some despise the gospel on account of its simplicity. Many at Corinth would seem to have done the same (*1 Cor.* 1:18, 23). Some of Paul's detractors may have criticised the simplicity of his approach, while they themselves made the gospel seem complicated to understand, perhaps in order to appear erudite. The gospel is not advice, but power. When advice is given, the importance we attach to it depends upon our understanding of the wisdom of the person who gives it. Paul, however, preached the gospel as the power of God (*Rom.* 1:16). He proclaimed it as the Word of God (*Col.* 1:25). It is likely that Paul's opponents tried to undermine the final authority of the Scriptures that he taught.

It is amazing how easily we may lose sight of the priority of the gospel and its simplicity. As churches we can become caught up with all kinds of programmes that in the end obscure our primary function to obey our Saviour's last commission. When we present the gospel, we may fail to present it clearly and simply, forgetting that it is God's power for the salvation of everyone who believes.

5. Lack of vigilance

Paul sensed that the Corinthians lacked caution and watchfulness. They 'put up with it readily enough' when someone preached a different Jesus and gospel, with a different spirit (v. 4). They may have prided themselves on their tolerance of different views. They may have allowed themselves to be impressed by the false teachers' 'lofty speech or wisdom', the very qualities Paul determined to avoid (*1 Cor.* 2:1). Instead of looking for the preaching of Jesus Christ and him crucified, as they had been taught to do, the Corinthians accepted teaching that did not have these fundamentals at its centre.

THE SOURCE OF THE DANGERS

1. Satan

As we have indicated, the primary source of all these dangers was, and is, Satan. Verse 3 provides this instruction. 'But I am afraid that as the serpent deceived Eve by his cunning, your thoughts will be led astray from a sincere and pure devotion to Christ.' For 'serpent' we may read 'Satan'. It is sadly possible to live as if Satan were a myth and to be totally unaware of his unceasing activity and amazing subtlety. Satan endeavours to draw men and women away from the love of truth and to embrace instead error. He takes them captive 'by philosophy and empty deceit'. He encourages attention and loyalty to human tradition and the basic principles of this world rather than to our Lord Jesus Christ (*Col.* 2:8).

2. 'Super-apostles'

The second source of danger came from the 'super-apostles', so-called, who were Satan's instruments. Paul declares, 'I consider that I am not in the least inferior to these super-apostles' (v. 5). In verse 13 Paul describes them in the original Greek as 'pseudo-apostles'. These were people who may have claimed to be 'super-apostles' or who were regarded as such by some Corinthian Christians. It appears they placed stress upon their eloquence and training, or, if they themselves did not do so, those who supported them did (v. 6). The implication of verse 7 is that they did not hesitate to require payment for their services. Paul asks, 'did I commit a sin in humbling myself so that you might be exalted, because I preached God's gospel to you free of charge?'

Super-apostles were unashamed of selling themselves and their services, copying the world's frequent pattern. It is not unusual for a company to charge more than all its competitors quite deliberately because of its conviction, often based upon research, that then people believe that they are the best. Paul's 'competitors' adopted a similar philosophy. If you charge people a lot, many are gullible enough to imagine that it is because you are the best. This, however, is not the manner in which Christians – and particularly Christian teachers and preachers – are to behave.

Super-apostles viewed themselves as superior to Paul and the other apostles. This in itself should have made the Corinthian believers suspicious. The New Testament does not allow us to overlook the uniqueness of the apostles and their teaching and preaching. The church is 'built on the foundation of the apostles and prophets, Christ Jesus himself being the cornerstone' (*Eph.* 2:20). The gospel the apostles delivered to men and women was what they themselves had first received from God (*1 Cor.* 15: 1–4). They were commissioned by God to give his Word in its fullness – the mystery kept hidden for ages and generations but now disclosed to God's people (*Col.* 1:25–26). They were privileged to make known the glorious riches of this mystery (*Col.* 1:27). No Christians following them in the course of history have inherited their unique authority. Their qualifications were supernatural. Once their work was done in delivering the truth of the gospel, it was perfectly written down and preserved in the infallible record of the New Testament. It is there for the church's benefit at every stage of her history.

Paul needed to speak against the super-apostles not for his own sake, but for the sake of the truth. 'As the truth of Christ is in me, this boasting of mine will not be silenced in the regions of Achaia' (v. 10). More important than eloquence and superior wisdom is knowledge. 'Even if I am unskilled in speaking, I am not so in knowledge; indeed, in every way we have made this plain to you in all things' (v. 6).

Concerning financial support, Paul knew it is better to give than to get. He explained this also as he said farewell to the Ephesian elders. 'In all things I have shown you that by working hard in this way we must help the weak and remember the words of the Lord Jesus, how he himself said, "It is more blessed to give than to receive"' (*Acts* 20:35). Paul explains why he had not demanded financial support but had preached the gospel to the Corinthians 'free of charge' (v. 7). We may learn once again from Paul's example that we should always be careful not to give cause for criticism of the way we administer finance in the church. We should take pains to do what is right, not only in the sight of God but also in the eyes of others (*2 Cor.* 8:20–21).

Paul raises the matter of finance by asking a question. 'Or did I commit a sin in humbling myself so that you might be exalted, because I preached God's gospel to you free of charge?'. It was in Corinth that Paul 'found a Jew named Aquila, a native of Pontus, recently come from Italy with his wife Priscilla, because Claudius had commanded all the Jews to leave Rome. And he went to see them, and because he was of the same trade he stayed with them and worked, for they were tentmakers by trade' (*Acts* 18:2–3). Paul used his tentmaking skills to pay his way.

The super-apostles suggested it was demeaning to work in such a manner and not to expect payment for preaching. Paul explains that, in effect, he 'robbed' other churches by receiving money from them to support his work in Corinth (v. 8). Even when in financial straits in Corinth, he had never been a charge upon their resources. Rather, Christians who came from Macedonia supplied what he needed. It was Paul's continuing purpose not to be a burden to the Corinthians in any way (v. 9). He was determined not to stop 'boasting' about this in the region of Achaia, not in order to exalt himself or because he did not love the Corinthians, but so that no one would lump him together with the so called 'super-apostles' (vv. 11–12).

THE TRUTH UNMASKED

Paul now uncovers the truth about the so-called 'super-apostles'. 'For such men are false apostles, deceitful workmen, disguising themselves as apostles of Christ' (v. 13). They are Satan's agents and instruments, reflecting the character of their master. 'Satan disguises himself as an angel of light' (v. 14). Such a description underlines his deceptiveness. Angels are envoys of God, and God himself is light. When Satan deceives, he gives every impression of bringing divine revelation. The end that awaits Satan awaits those who do his work (v. 15).

PAUL'S MOTIVATION

It is important that throughout this discussion of the dangers surrounding the Corinthians and the source of these difficulties, we recognise what Paul's motivation was in writing as he did. Verse 2 discloses it: 'I feel a divine jealousy for you, since I betrothed you to one husband, to present you as a pure virgin to Christ.' God is jealous for his people. He is zealous in his pursuit of what is for their good. This is a truth already revealed in the Old Testament (*Exod.* 20:5; 34:14; *Deut.* 4:24; 5:9; 6:15; *Josh.* 24:19). His jealousy springs from the unique sensitivity of his love. Paul was jealous over the Corinthians with God's own jealousy. Some might have thought Paul's concern 'foolishness', but it reflected God's concern for his people's love for his Son.

SPIRITUAL PRIORITIES

We gain the maximum value from this passage as we identify three spiritual priorities that emerge.

1. Devotion to Christ

The purity of our devotion to the Lord Jesus Christ is a spiritual priority. The language Paul uses in verses 2 and 3 indicates the amazingly intimate relationship we have as believers to the Lord Jesus. The complaint of the Lord Jesus in the Book of Revelation to the church at Ephesus was that they had forsaken their first love of him (*Rev.* 2:4). It is a miracle of God's grace that he unites us to the Lord Jesus. We are like those promised in marriage (v. 2). Our love for him matters, and matters intensely. Our faithfulness to the Lord Jesus is imperative. Satan sees to it that all kinds of things – even spiritual duties and activities – rival or threaten our love for the Lord Jesus. We should be jealous about the well-being of our love for him. We are never closer to God the Father than when we love his Son.

2. Watchfulness in listening

In view of Satan's unceasing activity, we are to be on our guard. He comes at us most frequently through our mind and its thoughts (v. 3). He may do it through people to whom we listen or books and magazines we read. The Book of Acts commends the Bereans, for even when the Apostle Paul came to them, they did not accept what he said without first checking it out from the Scriptures (*Acts* 17:11). Paul encourages the Corinthians to do the same, because that was an area in which they had been careless. 'For if someone comes and proclaims another Jesus than the one we proclaimed, or if you receive a different spirit from the one you received, or if you accept a different gospel from the one you accepted, you put up with it readily enough' (v. 4).

3. Discernment

Paul does not encourage the Corinthians to be suspicious of everyone, but he longs for them to be discerning. We are to prove all things, test everything and hold on to the good (*1 Thess.* 5:21). We are to check not only what we hear but the spirit and attitude of those who may seek to influence us (v. 4). Rather than being impressed

[111]

by eloquence or training, we should look above all for 'the meekness and gentleness of Christ' (*2 Cor.* 10:1). Satan's ability to masquerade as 'an angel of light', and his agents 'as servants of righteousness', means that to be forewarned should mean to be forearmed. 'The prudent sees danger and hides himself, but the simple go on and suffer for it' (*Prov.* 27:12).

18

Boasting and Its Perils

[16]I repeat, let no one think me foolish. But even if you do, accept me as a fool, so that I too may boast a little. [17]What I am saying with this boastful confidence, I say not with the Lord's authority but as a fool. [18]Since many boast according to the flesh, I too will boast. [19]For you gladly bear with fools, being wise yourselves! [20]For you bear it if someone makes slaves of you, or devours you, or takes advantage of you, or puts on airs, or strikes you in the face. [21]To my shame, I must say, we were too weak for that!

But whatever anyone else dares to boast of—I am speaking as a fool—I also dare to boast of that. [22]Are they Hebrews? So am I. Are they Israelites? So am I. Are they offspring of Abraham? So am I. [23]Are they servants of Christ? I am a better one—I am talking like a madman—with far greater labours, far more imprisonments, with countless beatings, and often near death. [24]Five times I received at the hands of the Jews the forty lashes less one. [25]Three times I was beaten with rods. Once I was stoned. Three times I was shipwrecked; a night and a day I was adrift at sea; [26]on frequent journeys, in danger from rivers, danger from robbers, danger from my own people, danger from Gentiles, danger in the city, danger in the wilderness, danger at sea, danger from false brothers; [27]in toil and hardship, through many a sleepless night, in hunger and thirst, often without food, in cold and exposure. [28]And, apart from other things, there is the daily pressure on me of my anxiety for all the churches. [29]Who is weak, and I am not weak? Who is made to fall, and I am not indignant?

[30]If I must boast, I will boast of the things that show my weakness. [31]The God and Father of the Lord Jesus, he who

is blessed forever, knows that I am not lying. [32]At Damascus, the governor under King Aretas was guarding the city of Damascus in order to seize me, [33]but I was let down in a basket through a window in the wall and escaped his hands (2 Cor. 11:16–33).

Paul continues to answer his critics, some of whom were false teachers who exercised an influence in Corinth. The first fifteen verses of the chapter indicate that these antagonists were not afraid of setting themselves up as important and of parading their training and knowledge (vv. 5–6).

They plainly boasted of their superiority, and without justification. Many Corinthians were so taken in by these 'super-apostles' that they put up with them even though exploited by them (v. 20).

CHARACTERISTICS OF FALSE TEACHING

Verse 20 provides three characteristics of false teaching, seen in many contemporary cults. Paul writes, 'For you bear it if someone makes slaves of you, or devours you, or takes advantage of you, or puts on airs, or strikes you in the face.'

The first characteristic is *enslavement*. In subtle ways false teachers demand such a degree of loyalty from those they teach, that those who listen to them become slaves to rules and regulations that go far beyond what the Bible teaches. False teachers frequently dictate what their adherents may or may not do.

The second characteristic is *exploitation*. Sadly, it is possible in human relationships to be manipulative and even to use others for selfish and unworthy ends or purposes. False teachers may tell people, for instance, what they must do with their money and, in urging generosity, really be feathering their own nest. The exploitation may sometimes be sexual, as when individuals use counselling – so called – to get close to people in need, only then to abuse the privilege.

The third characteristic is *ill treatment*. The rule of false teachers may go beyond the bounds of the control that any individual should ever have over another person. People may be so taken in by what they regard as 'charismatic' leadership and spiritual authority that they accept anything.

Paul never did to the Corinthians what the 'super-apostles' did. He never enslaved them. The allegiance he wanted from them was not to himself but to the Lord Jesus. He never exploited or took advantage of them, but rather worked with his hands so that he looked for no financial support from them. Sarcastically he adds, 'To my shame, I must say, we were too weak for that!' (v. 21)

CRAZY TALK

Paul decides to take on his opponents on their own terms by indulging himself in boasting. 'I repeat, let no one think me foolish. But even if you do, accept me as a fool, so that I too may boast a little' (v. 16). He recognises straightaway that self-confident boasting is foreign to spirituality. 'What I am saying with this boastful confidence, I say not with the Lord's authority but as a fool' (v. 17). He boasts only to show the truth about his situation and that of his opponents.

SPECIFIC BOASTS OF PAUL'S OPPONENTS

Two areas of boasting in which Paul's opponents engaged appear in verses 21– 29 and yet others in the next chapter. *First, they boasted about their Jewishness* (v. 22). That this was the case indicates that they were probably Judaisers who made much of circumcision. Such are found elsewhere in the New Testament churches, and particular reference is made to them in the letter to the Galatians.

Circumcision became a matter of controversy in the early church because the first Christians – who were Jews – required the circumcision of Gentile believers (*Acts* 15:1). The Council at Jerusalem resolved the issue (*Acts* 15:1– 21), when it agreed that it should not be obligatory for Gentiles. However, there remained those of 'the circumcision party', or Judaisers, who still hankered after such a requirement (*Gal.* 2:12, *Titus* 1:10).

Second, Paul's opponents boasted about their service for Christ (v. 23). Presumably they bragged about the extent of their work and what they had suffered in its cause. Paul answers with boasts that more than matched those of the false teachers, the 'super-apostles', although admitting at once, as we have indicated, the foolishness of boasting (v. 21).

Paul begins by pointing out that there was no doubt about his own Jewish ancestry and essential Jewishness. As he shared with the Philippians, he had more grounds for boasting of Jewish descent and faithfulness than most. He was 'circumcised on the eighth day, of the people of Israel, of the tribe of Benjamin, a Hebrew of Hebrews; as to the law, a Pharisee; as to zeal, a persecutor of the church; as to righteousness under the law, blameless' (*Phil.* 3:5–6).

Paul then matches the false teachers' boasts about their service of Christ with a catalogue of his own. First, no-one's volume of work in the interests of the kingdom of the Lord Jesus was greater. He had 'far greater labours' (v. 23) – although again, he acknowledges that to make such a claim is foolish!

Second, he had been subjected to danger more than most. He had been imprisoned, flogged, exposed to death, beaten, stoned and shipwrecked (vv. 23– 25). Constantly on the move, in the city, in the country or at sea, he had been in peril on rivers, from robbers, Jews, Gentiles and false brothers (v. 26).

Third, his physical hardships exceeded those of others, for he knew what it was to go without sleep, to be hungry and thirsty, cold and exposed (v. 27).

Fourth, and significantly, the greatest burden he bore, far exceeding any other, was the pastoral and spiritual care of the churches. This brought him the greatest cost as he indicates by the phrase 'apart from other things' (v. 28).

Paul felt deeply his identity with God's people, as any true pastor does (v. 29). When others were desperate, he entered into their desperation. When someone succumbed to Satan's temptations, Paul was angry with Satan and concerned for the sinner. Part of our hidden, but often most significant, service of the Lord Jesus is struggling in prayer for others, and especially those for whom we have spiritual responsibility.

Again Paul indicates his keen sensitivity to the foolishness of boasting (v. 30). To counter that folly, he determines that if he must boast, then it will be about the events that show his weakness rather than his strength. At the same time, he affirms his truthfulness before God in what he says (v. 31). The example he gives of weakness was his somewhat undignified escape from Damascus in a basket (vv. 32–33; cf. *Acts* 9:23– 25). Paul will continue to counter the boasts of his opponents in the next section of the letter.

BENEFICIAL LESSONS

Sad though this conflict with his detractors was, it is important to pause and consider what helpful conclusions we may draw from this passage. It is here for our instruction, and we may pinpoint seven lessons.

First, boasting is always dangerous (v. 16). Once we start, we may get carried away by it. Pride never completely dies in us, and once given opportunity it quickly moves out of control.

Second, self-confident boasting is stupid (v. 17). Boasting of this kind is the way of the world, for the world encourages us to sell ourselves (v. 18). When we recognise that 'From him and through him and to him are all things' (*Rom.* 11:36), we shudder at any thought or suggestion of ascribing to ourselves what belongs to God.

Third, our concern in speaking about ourselves and our achievements must be to talk as the Lord would have us talk (v. 17). Then we 'do nothing from rivalry or conceit, but in humility count others more significant than yourselves (*Phil.* 2:3).

Fourth, Christian service must be marked by unselfishness. We may achieve this as we deliberately follow the example of our Lord Jesus in his 'meekness and gentleness' (v. 20; cf. *2 Cor.* 10:1, *Phil.* 2:5– 11). It is better to be regarded as weak than selfish or manipulative (v. 21).

Fifth, there is no place in the Christian life for confidence in human achievements or ancestry (v. 22). Essential to spiritual understanding and entering into salvation is the absolute poverty of all we have to offer God, and our one-hundred-percent dependence upon his grace and mercy.

Sixth, there is no place for confidence in the volume of our service (v. 23). At best, we are but unprofitable servants! The last words of William Grimshaw, an outstanding eighteenth-century Christian, were appropriately, 'Here goes an unprofitable servant.' The best we may do is a poor response to the love of our Lord Jesus in going to the cross for us.

Finally, we all have weaknesses, whatever our strengths. We do better, therefore, to boast of what shows our weakness than our strength, for then we confess our dependence upon God. God is not honoured by boasting, but he is by humble dependence upon him.

19

Paul's Vision and His Thorn

¹I must go on boasting. Though there is nothing to be gained by it, I will go on to visions and revelations of the Lord. ²I know a man in Christ who fourteen years ago was caught up to the third heaven—whether in the body or out of the body I do not know, God knows. ³And I know that this man was caught up into paradise—whether in the body or out of the body I do not know, God knows— ⁴and he heard things that cannot be told, which man may not utter. ⁵On behalf of this man I will boast, but on my own behalf I will not boast, except of my weaknesses. ⁶Though if I should wish to boast, I would not be a fool, for I would be speaking the truth. But I refrain from it, so that no one may think more of me than he sees in me or hears from me. ⁷So to keep me from becoming conceited because of the surpassing greatness of the revelations, a thorn was given me in the flesh, a messenger of Satan to harass me, to keep me from becoming conceited. ⁸Three times I pleaded with the Lord about this, that it should leave me. ⁹But he said to me, 'My grace is sufficient for you, for my power is made perfect in weakness.' Therefore I will boast all the more gladly of my weaknesses, so that the power of Christ may rest upon me. ¹⁰ For the sake of Christ, then, I am content with weaknesses, insults, hardships, persecutions, and calamities. For when I am weak, then I am strong.

¹¹I have been a fool! You forced me to it, for I ought to have been commended by you. For I was not at all inferior to these super-apostles, even though I am nothing. ¹²The signs of a true apostle were performed among you with utmost patience, with signs and wonders and mighty works. ¹³For in what were you less favored than the rest of the churches, except that I myself did not burden you? Forgive me this wrong! (2 Cor. 12:1–13).

Paul continues his theme of boasting. 'I must go on boasting' v. 1). In the previous sections his boasting focused upon his Jewishness and his service for the Lord Jesus Christ. These were two areas in which his detractors obviously criticised him. However, there were others, and he mentions two more.

SPIRITUAL EXPERIENCES

1 Corinthians 12–14 indicates that the Corinthians were particularly interested and intrigued by the more spectacular and unusual gifts of the Holy Spirit. The promoting of this preoccupying interest may have been the emphasis of the 'super-apostles'.

Again Paul replies by boasting of his own spiritual experiences, and especially of 'visions and revelations of the Lord' (v. 1). We must notice, however, that he renews his qualification about the value of such boasting: 'there is nothing to be gained' from it (v. 1). Boasting about spiritual experiences is especially inappropriate, since if they are genuine, they are God's gift, and completely so. Boasting so easily arises from pride, and it serves to increase pride. Once we start boasting, we inevitably separate ourselves from others and sow seeds of disunity. Proud we separate, humble we stay together.

Pride is very much a secret sin. The people we consider to be humble and immune from pride are probably most aware of its snare. They know that the only One who can possibly humble them and keep them so is their Master, as he shows them its foolishness and sets before them his example of humility.

Paul describes a man he knew in Christ (v. 2). He clearly refers to himself, but this way of writing in the third person is an expression of humility. He wants to share the experience, but he does not want to focus attention upon himself. Fourteen years before the writing of this letter, he was 'caught up to the third heaven' (v. 2). He did not know if it was in the body or out of the body. He did not know if it was solely a spiritual experience or perhaps also a physical one. He was caught up to paradise (vv. 3–4). 'Paradise' is an oriental word, first used by the Persians, of an enclosure or a walled garden. It expresses the idea of a place of supreme happiness above the earth. 'The tree of life' is spoken of as being in the paradise of God (*Rev.* 2:7). Our Lord Jesus indicated that it is the heavenly home to which the spirits of believers go at death (*Luke* 23:43).

Caught up into paradise, Paul heard inexpressible things that he was not permitted to tell. The experience – in human reckoning – was worth bragging about, but he determined not to do so (v. 6). (This underlines the suggestion we have made about why he writes in the third person to describe it.) Rather, his determination was to boast only about his weaknesses (v. 5). When we boast about our weaknesses, we boast about how great God is to use such feeble instruments! Paul did not deny that – humanly speaking – he had plenty about which to boast. However, he did not want anyone to think of him more highly than was appropriate to the integrity of his life and speech.

Verse 7 clearly confirms that the 'man in Christ' in verse 2 was Paul himself. He had received revelations of 'surpassing greatness' (v. 7). Such spiritual experiences, however, brought the peril of spiritual pride, which is one of the worst forms that pride can take. It indicates that we have lost sight of the cross and our dependence upon the grace of our Lord Jesus Christ. There is nothing good that the devil does not try to turn to evil. When we are closest to God, Satan may attack us with both subtle and obvious temptations.

To curb Paul's pride, to keep him from becoming conceited, he was given 'a thorn' in the flesh (v. 7). We are nowhere told what this thorn was. It was physical, since it is described as being in his 'flesh'. Much speculation has surrounded it. However, it is not helpful to speculate, and its identity is probably hidden for good reasons. What we do know is that it 'harassed' him, implying the regularity and intensity of the problems it caused.

The 'thorn' became 'a messenger of Satan' (v. 7). No doubt Satan whispered when the problem was most acute, 'Why you, Paul? Without it you would be able to serve God so much better. Why should God allow this to happen to you?' In tempting us, Satan encourages us to doubt the integrity of God's character and promises. If he can succeed in his attacks on our faith, we soon fail to live as Christians in other areas of life. When acute problems bother us, he particularly tries to cast doubt upon God's love.

Paul describes his spiritual struggle with the Lord about his 'thorn' (v. 8). Three times he pleaded with the Lord to remove it. This brings to mind the way in which our Lord Jesus prayed three times in Gethsemane that the bitter cup of suffering before him might be removed (*Matt.* 26:36–44). The Lord's answer to Paul's prayer was 'No'. Instead, he was to bear it, and he would be given the necessary grace and strength.

This was a truth Paul had already taught the Corinthians in his first letter. 'No temptation has overtaken you that is not common to man. God is faithful, and he will not let you be tempted beyond your ability, but with the temptation he will also provide the way of escape, that you may be able to endure it' (*1 Cor.* 10:13). The 'way of escape', more often than not, is a renewed experience of our Saviour's grace. Instead of taking the thorn away from Paul, the Lord promised, 'My grace is sufficient for you, for my power is made perfect in weakness' (v. 9). As Ambrose, a fourth-century Christian, put it, 'Sometimes when Satan is most busy, the Lord steps in with his own testimony and stops the lion's mouth that he can say no more.'

How priceless a promise verse 9 is for every Christian! How rewarding is any 'thorn' that teaches this lesson! Some important lessons may never be learned without 'thorns' (*e.g., 2 Cor.* 1:3–11). The Lord's promise and gracious reassurance altered and transformed Paul's whole attitude to the suffering God permitted in his life. It taught him not to boast in his strength or strengths, but in his weakness and weaknesses (v. 9). In this glorious paradox he discovered the secret of blessing – Christ's power then rested on him (v. 9). That was why, for Christ's sake, he delighted in weaknesses, insults, hardships, persecutions, and difficulties. When he was weak, then he was strong (v. 10).

This principle is neither new nor unique to the New Testament. Isaiah declares that God 'gives power to the faint, and to him who has no might he increases strength' (40:29). Paul's words are an application of the principle of 2 Corinthians 4:7: 'But we have this treasure in jars of clay, to show that the surpassing power belongs to God and not to us.' It is the natural consequence of God's deliberate choice of 'what is weak in the world to shame the strong' (*1 Cor.* 1:27). This is a principle by which to live! God makes all Satan's temp-tations promote our good as they cause us to turn in prayerful dependence to God and his promises. As we are humbled by our difficulties, so we are strengthened by our Saviour's all-sufficient grace.

PROOFS OF APOSTLESHIP

Paul draws attention now to the proofs of his apostleship (vv. 11–13). Clearly this subject was an issue among the Corinthians, for some of Paul's opponents and detractors claimed to be 'super-apostles'. There is no such position in the church, although human pride and wisdom may think differently. In drawing attention to his apostleship, Paul again indicates the stupidity of boasting. The truth was that it ought to have been the Corinthians who stood up for Paul rather than for him to have to defend himself (v. 11). The Corinthians were in a special position to commend Paul because they had witnessed 'the signs of a true apostle' during his eighteen months among them, the period when the church was established in Corinth. They were living letters of testimonial to his apostleship.

Paul identifies 'signs and wonders and mighty works' as some of the marks of his apostleship. He probably points to these because such evidences were regarded as crucial by the 'super-apostles'. He had performed them among them 'with utmost patience' (v. 12). Significantly, Acts 18:1–18 records none of these acts of power. This implies they were not the most important marks of apostleship. The Corinthians, however, foolishly influenced by the 'super-apostles', regarded them as such.

The importance of the apostles lay in their teaching, in their faithful delivery of the gospel according to the Scriptures (*1 Cor.* 15:1–9, *Acts* 18:11; 20:27). The purpose of 'signs and wonders and mighty works' (v.12) was to confirm the Word that was preached (*Mark* 16:20, *Heb.* 2:3–4). The only thing Paul failed to do – that he might justifiably have chosen to do – was to be a financial burden to them (v. 13). Paul therefore apologises!

SALUTARY PRIORITIES

Helpful lessons emerge from Paul's baring of his soul to the Corinthians.

Spiritual experience

More important than special – and perhaps exciting – spiritual experiences is the daily experience of our Saviour's grace. Claims about spiritual experiences are not to be taken at face value: they are always to be judged and tested by the clear teaching of the Bible.

While spiritual experiences may come to us at special meetings, they are just as likely, if not more so, through our proving God's promises in tough situations or in suffering. Knowing God is more important than experience-seeking. Knowing him is more important than spiritual gifts. The best test of spiritual growth and health is our desire to know God.

Weakness and strength
Essential to true wisdom is the recognition of our weakness. Weakness is a distinct theme in both 1 and 2 Corinthians (*1 Cor.* 1:26–31, *2 Cor.* 4:7; 12:9–10). Paradoxically, our weakness is an asset.

The challenge of difficulties
Paul shares the challenge that came to him through many kinds of difficulty, including weakness, hardships, and persecutions (v. 10). Our Lord Jesus made sure that the ever-present difficulties that accompany discipleship are not in small print (*Luke* 9:57–62). Difficulties are inevitable for Christians wherever they live in the world. But so what? God is the same wherever we may be. As David Livingstone put it, 'What are difficulties but to be surmounted?' We may find it easier to walk with Jesus when we have difficulties, as Paul did. Samuel Wilkes, an eighteenth-century Christian, aptly observed, 'A Christian never falls asleep in the fire or in the water, but grows drowsy in the sunshine.' Difficulties show how securely anchored we are in our faith in God. Hudson Taylor, a nineteenth-century missionary to China, spoke of a challenge that faced him and his fellow missionaries. 'I have found that there are three stages. First, it is impossible, then it is difficult, then it is done'. Our philosophy needs to be the same.

Stand up for God's servants
Satan sees to it that the very best of Christ's servants will be criticised and sometimes maligned, as Paul was. If the Corinthians had stood up for him, as they ought to have done, much of this second letter would not have needed to be written. When people speak evil of those whom we know to be true servants of Christ, we should not be silent. Rather we should with 'the meekness and gentleness of Christ' (*2 Cor.* 10:1) try to put the record straight.

Appropriate boasting

While it was again necessary for Paul to defend himself against false accusations so that the Corinthians' faith in the apostolic testimony should not be undermined, he knew that boasting was foolish. The only boasting that is appropriate is boasting in the Lord. Such boasting is a blessing to others, whereas boasting in ourselves is the opposite. David's determination may be ours: 'My soul makes its boast in the LORD; let the humble hear and be glad' (*Psa.* 34:2).

20

Preparing the Ground for a Third Visit

[14]Here for the third time I am ready to come to you. And I will not be a burden, for I seek not what is yours but you. For children are not obligated to save up for their parents, but parents for their children. [15]I will most gladly spend and be spent for your souls. If I love you more, am I to be loved less? [16]But granting that I myself did not burden you, I was crafty, you say, and got the better of you by deceit. [17]Did I take advantage of you through any of those whom I sent to you? [18]I urged Titus to go, and sent the brother with him. Did Titus take advantage of you? Did we not act in the same spirit? Did we not take the same steps?

[19]Have you been thinking all along that we have been defending ourselves to you? It is in the sight of God that we have been speaking in Christ, and all for your upbuilding, beloved. [20]For I fear that perhaps when I come I may find you not as I wish, and that you may find me not as you wish—that perhaps there may be quarreling, jealousy, anger, hostility, slander, gossip, conceit, and disorder. [21]I fear that when I come again my God may humble me before you, and I may have to mourn over many of those who sinned earlier and have not repented of the impurity, sexual immorality, and sensuality that they have practiced.

[1]This is the third time I am coming to you. Every charge must be established by the evidence of two or three witnesses. [2]I warned those who sinned before and all the others, and I warn them now while absent, as I did when present on my second visit, that if I come again I will not spare them— [3]since you seek proof that Christ is speaking in me. He is not weak

in dealing with you, but is powerful among you. ⁴For he was crucified in weakness, but lives by the power of God. For we also are weak in him, but in dealing with you we will live with him by the power of God.

⁵Examine yourselves, to see whether you are in the faith. Test yourselves. Or do you not realize this about yourselves, that Jesus Christ is in you?—unless indeed you fail to meet the test! ⁶I hope you will find out that we have not failed the test. ⁷But we pray to God that you may not do wrong—not that we may appear to have met the test, but that you may do what is right, though we may seem to have failed. ⁸For we cannot do anything against the truth, but only for the truth. ⁹For we are glad when we are weak and you are strong. Your restoration is what we pray for. ¹⁰For this reason I write these things while I am away from you, that when I come I may not have to be severe in my use of the authority that the Lord has given me for building up and not for tearing down.

¹¹Finally, brothers, rejoice. Aim for restoration, comfort one another, agree with one another, live in peace; and the God of love and peace will be with you. ¹²Greet one another with a holy kiss. ¹³All the saints greet you.

¹⁴The grace of the Lord Jesus Christ and the love of God and the fellowship of the Holy Spirit be with you all (2 Cor. 12:14–13:14).

Twice Paul mentions his proposed 'third visit' (12:14; 13:1). Part of his intention in writing this letter is to prepare the way for it. It is for this reason that he continues to write honestly about the relationship of himself and his colleagues to the Corinthians. We may identify seven purposes in the concluding part of his letter.

NO CHANGE IN FINANCIAL POLICY

First, there is to be no change in policy regarding financial support (12:14–18). Paul expresses his determination to hold on to his practice of not being a financial burden to the Corinthians (12:14). As we saw earlier, his practice of maintaining his financial independence, where he felt it wise, was misunderstood or misinterpreted by some at Corinth.

The different practice of the 'super-apostles' almost certainly prompted this criticism. We can imagine the pernicious suggestion that was made, 'If Paul were a genuine apostle, he would demand financial support.' They may even have quoted the words of the Lord Jesus to back up their suggestion: 'The labourer deserves his wages' (*Luke* 10:7). However, Paul practised another principle that the Lord Jesus taught, 'It is more blessed to give than to receive' (*Acts* 20:35).

Paul wanted it to be plain that it was not the material possessions of the Corinthians that he was interested in, but their spiritual well-being (12:14). Paul was the spiritual father of many of them. He reminds them of a human principle that has spiritual relevance and application: 'children are not obligated to save up for their parents, but parents for their children' (12:14). Parents should be prepared to make sacrifices for their children rather than the other way round. Holding to this principle in its spiritual application, Paul determined to spend everything he had, if necessary, for the Corinthians, as well as giving himself and all his energies to them (12:15). With such a determination, he followed in his Master's footsteps.

Sadly, as a result of the insinuations of Paul's detractors, his endeavours to do the right and best thing for the Corinthians only inclined them to love him less (12:15). Satan's activity was behind such a sad circumstance. However, the possibility that the Corinthians might love him less was no reason for Paul departing from a right principle (12:16). Some members of the church may have used Paul's refusal to demand financial support to suggest he was engaged in subtle trickery. He answers this possible suggestion by drawing attention to the integrity of those he sent to Corinth to administer the gifts for the poor saints at Jerusalem. Titus and the brother who accompanied him were in complete harmony with Paul's motives and actions (12:18).

It is natural and right not to want our good to be spoken of in an evil manner (*Rom.* 14:16). If it is, however, that is no reason to stop doing what is right. If we cease pursuing what is good and the best, Satan has won a victory. As we sometimes say, 'Two wrongs do not make a right.'

A CLEAR SPIRITUAL OBJECTIVE

Second, Paul expresses his spiritual objective of upbuilding the Corinthians in their faith (12:19). He was sensitive to the thought of the Corinthians imagining that his letter was purely a form of self-defence. His indulging in boasting accentuated this fear. So he asks, 'Have you been thinking all along that we have been defending ourselves to you?' Part of pastoral sensitivity is the desire and ability to put ourselves in the position of those we want to help and to imagine what they may be thinking.

Paul assures the Corinthians that he and those whom he represents have been speaking and writing 'in the sight of God' and 'in Christ' (12:19). Both phrases – 'in the sight of God' and 'in Christ' – are worthy of thought and emphasis. To act remembering that God sees everything we do, and that we are to live in the light of our spiritual union with Christ, are secrets of holiness and integrity. Paul affirms that his basic objective was that the Corinthians should be built up in their faith (12:19). In secular use 'upbuilding' has to do with the erection of a building. It is used here and elsewhere in the New Testament of building people up spiritually. Church growth is not just a matter of numbers. With growth in numbers there must be growth in grace and in the knowledge of the Lord Jesus. As the church grows spiritually, she is equipped to grow numerically (*Acts* 9:31). It is a secret of effective evangelism. The strengthening of believers is a continuing purpose of pastoral care.

APPREHENSIONS AND FEARS

Third, Paul puts into words his apprehensions and fears about his arrival in Corinth (12:20–21). He is anxious about the proposed visit. He is worried about their expectations of each other, of what he will find when he gets there, and what his feelings will be as a consequence. He is afraid that when he arrives, the Corinthians will not be as he wants them to be. They, in turn, may not find him to be to their liking. As to what he may find on his arrival, he is afraid of unearthing unpleasant and unresolved problems. Expressing his concerns in this way is a gentle means of encouraging the Corinthians to deal with unresolved issues before his arrival so that the visit may be a mutual encouragement.

Quarrels, jealousy, outbursts of anger, hostility, slander, gossip, conceit and disorder were some of the problems he anticipated. *Quarrels* quickly arise when human personalities are given the place that the Lord Jesus alone should occupy (cf. *1 Cor.* 1:12–13; 3:3–5) or when disputes get out of hand (*1 Cor.* 6:1–8). Once started, quarrels are not easily stopped. 'The beginning of strife is like letting out water, so quit before the quarrel breaks out.' (*Prov.* 17:14).

Jealousy is frequently behind quarrels, and leads to strife (*1 Cor.* 3:3). It prompts intrigue and false accusation (*Dan.* 6:4–5). Sadly it can operate even among Christian preachers and leaders (*Phil.* 1:15–18). 'Envy makes the bones rot' (*Prov.* 14:30).

Outbursts of anger flow from jealousy. Once anger bursts out, truth is easily lost sight of, and the devil gains the advantage. People then predictably take sides with the different parties to the argument, and *hostilities* or factions form. The protagonists then become the subject of *slander* and *gossip*, activities sadly enjoyed all too much by our fallen sinful nature. 'The words of a whisperer (or gossip) are like delicious morsels; they go down into the inner parts of the body' (*Prov.* 26:22).

Both slander and gossip display human *conceit*, for we then quickly slip into judging others (*Luke* 6:37). These unhappy acts of our sinful nature bring further sad *disorder*. All are contrary to the fruit of the Spirit, and all grieve him.

The prospect of facing such issues made Paul fearful. He would be humbled by them. He would be grieved beyond words at the failure to repent of those who had sinned (12:21). 'Impurity, sexual immorality and sensuality' express a sad retrogression. Sexual sin begins in the mind with impure thoughts. Impurity of thought leads to sexual sin. Unchecked, sexual sin leads to increasingly uncontrolled sexual excess.

Paul's sharing of his fears must have stimulated God-fearing believers at Corinth to put their house in order before his arrival.

THE NECESSITY OF SPIRITUAL DISCIPLINE

Fourth, Paul confirms the necessity of the spiritual discipline he must exercise when he arrives in Corinth (13:1–4). It was impossible for Paul, first, as an apostle, and, secondly, as the first evangelist and pastor of the Corinthian Christians, to visit them without endeavouring to put right whatever he found wrong.

There were God-given principles to apply, and this is always the case. One was that of Deuteronomy 19:15: 'A single witness shall not suffice against a person for any crime or for any wrong in connection with any offense that he has committed. Only on the evidence of two witnesses or of three witnesses shall a charge be established' (cf. *2 Cor.* 13:1). We need to recognise the relevance of the Old Testament to New Testament believers. Paul was determined not to act hastily but with proper care and attention to the issues involved.

The apostle repeats a warning he gave the Corinthians on his second visit. He would not spare those who sinned earlier or any others who had done so similarly since (13:2). His necessary action would prove that he spoke by Christ's power (13:3) – something that his detractors no doubt denied. The Corinthians needed to appreciate that in dealing with the apostle they were dealing with the Lord Jesus himself, since Paul was his representative.

Some might have suggested that Paul and his colleagues were weak or appeared feeble (13:3–4). Paul's answer is simple yet profound. The example of our Saviour who died and hung upon a cross in such apparent weakness should make us beware of misreading or misunderstanding apparent weakness. The Lord Jesus is never feeble towards his people, but strong. So, too, are those who properly exercise pastoral care as his representatives. They are strong in him to do whatever is necessary. They are given all of Christ's power to accomplish what he calls them to do. Furthermore, the Lord Jesus is at work by his Spirit in those for whom they care!

THE IMPORTANCE OF SELF-EXAMINATION

Fifth, Paul urges upon the Corinthians the necessity of self-examination (13:5–6). The accusations and innuendoes against Paul and his colleagues necessarily prompted them to examine themselves and their personal adherence to the faith and the genuineness of their spiritual experience. That exercise of self-examination, however, was equally necessary for the Corinthians, as for us all. Paul is not urging unhealthy introspection. That suggestion is a lie Satan often encourages in order to put us off the necessary exercise. Just as we may regularly have medical checks, so we need to look ourselves over on the inside from time to time.

We are to test ourselves to see whether we are 'in the faith' (13:5) – that is to say, to check that we are genuinely 'born again'. The three tests of 1 John – faith in the Lord Jesus as the Christ (*1 John* 5:1), righteousness of life (*1 John* 2:29) and love for other believers (*1 John* 3:14) are fundamental evidences. Such testing was relevant to the 'super-apostles' also. Paul readily admits the priority of such self-examination on the part of himself and his colleagues (13:6).

Self-examination properly humbles us and reminds us of our absolute dependence upon the saving work of our Lord Jesus. The wisest self-examination is done as we examine ourselves in the light of what God teaches in his Word. Besides doing this when we are aware of a particular need to do so, we may do it every time we read and hear the Scriptures. Self-examination must result in action, otherwise it is dangerous. To discover that we are in the wrong and to do nothing about it accentuates the wrong and our responsibility for it. Self-examination is especially necessary if we judge others (*Luke* 6:41–42).

A PRAYER AND A LONGING

Sixth Paul shares his prayer and longing for them (13:7–10). His prayer is that God will keep the Corinthians from wrong. His motive is not to draw attention to his successful ministry among them; it is the honour of God and the well-being of the Corinthians. Paul's responsibility was not to be concerned for his own reputation but for the truth (13:8).

'The truth' is a way of expressing 'the gospel', the good news of our Lord Jesus. It is particularly appropriate because he himself is the truth (*John* 14:6; cf. *2 John* 1). The truth may be said to live in us as believers, and we are to walk in the truth (*2 John* 2,4). Walking in the truth is synonymous with living in obedience to God's commands, and especially his command that we love one another (*2 John* 6).

As Paul and his colleagues prayed for the Corinthians, they prayed for their spiritual maturity, whatever the cost of the achievement of that goal to those who served them (13:9).

Paul longed that his visit would not mean taking the Corinthians apart when he arrived, but rather putting them together. His motive in preparing the ground for his third visit was not the pulling down of the Corinthians but their upbuilding (13:10). He wanted his visit o be memorable for its encouragement, not for discouragement. His example reminds us that authority should never be exercised harshly, but gently and purposefully, for the encouragement of God's people in their relationship with him.

FINAL WORDS

Paul ends his letter with exhortations, a greeting and a prayerful wish (13:11–14). There are four exhortations in verse 11. First, 'aim for restoration' or perfection. We are to determine to grow in Christ, and in Christlikeness. Second, 'Listen to my appeal' (margin). 'Appeal' is a gentle word. Paul does not use the word 'order' or 'command' – as well he might have done as an apostle – in keeping with his desire to avoid harshness (13:10). Third, 'Agree with one another'. When as believers we strive to think in the same way, God the Holy Spirit is always present to enable us to have the mind of Christ in us. Fourth, 'Live in peace'. To live in peace requires effort (*Eph.* 4:3). Paul guarantees that with obedience to these imperatives, God's blessing will come (13:11). Where love and peace exist, God is present. Nothing hinders our experience of God's presence more than the absence of love and peace among us.

The greeting is first one they were to extend to one another. 'Greet one another with a holy kiss' (13:12). That kiss was intended to be a symbol of love and peace. It was to be a *holy* kiss. A kiss was the regular greeting in first-century society. The word 'holy' reminds us that a kiss could easily be abused, especially if men and women kissed one another. J. B. Phillips translates it, 'A hand-shake all round, please.' Paul then conveys to the Corinthians the greetings of all the believers with whom he and they were associated in the Lord Jesus (13:13).

BOTH A WISH AND A PRAYER

Paul's final words constitute not only a wish but a prayer. 'The grace of the Lord Jesus Christ, and the love of God, and the fellowship of the Holy Spirit be with you all' (13:14). Used so often as a final prayer of benediction among Christians, and sometimes said aloud in unison, these words constitute one of the loveliest and most meaningful prayers of the New Testament. We pray, first, for the grace of our Saviour's forgiveness, presence and strength. We pray, secondly, for the knowledge, assurance, experience and power of God the Father's love. Thirdly, we pray for the fellowship of the Holy Spirit as our Counsellor, the fellowship of his intercession, and the fellowship into which he desires to bring us with the Father and the Son, and with one another. It is a prayer to use and treasure, and upon which often to meditate.

Group Study Guide

This Study Guide has been prepared for group Bible study, but it can also be used individually. Those who use it on their own may find it helpful to keep a notebook of their responses.

The way in which group Bible studies are led can greatly enhance their value. A well-conducted study will appear as though it has been easy to lead, but that is usually because the leader has worked hard and planned well. Clear aims are essential.

AIMS

In all Bible study, individual or corporate, we have several aims:

1. To gain an understanding of the original meaning of the particular passage of Scripture;

2. To apply this to ourselves and our own situation;

3. To develop some specific ways of putting the biblical teaching into practice.

2 Timothy 3:16–17 provides a helpful structure. Paul says that Scripture is useful for:

  (i)   teaching us;

  (ii)   rebuking us;

  (iii) correcting, or changing us;

  (iv) training us in righteousness.

Consequently, in studying any passage of Scripture, we should always have in mind these questions:

What does this passage teach us (about God, ourselves, etc.)?

Does it rebuke us in some way?

How can its teaching transform us?

What equipment does it give us for serving Christ?

In fact, these four questions alone would provide a safe guide in any Bible study.

PRINCIPLES

In group Bible study we meet in order to learn about God's Word and ways 'with all the saints' *(Eph.* 3:18). But our own experience, as well as Scripture, tells us that the saints are not always what they *are* called to be in every situation – including group Bible study! Leaders ordinarily have to work hard and prepare well if the work of the group is to be spiritually profitable. The following guidelines for leaders may help to make this a reality.

[136]

Preparation:

1. Study and understand the passage yourself. The better prepared and more sure of the direction of the study you are, the more likely it is that the group will have a beneficial and enjoyable study.
Ask: What are the main things this passage is saying? How can this be made clear? This is not the same question as the more common 'What does this passage "say to you"?' which expects a reaction rather than an exposition of the passage. Be clear about that distinction yourself, and work at making it clear in the group study.

2. On the basis of your own study form a clear idea *before* the group meets of (i) the main theme(s) of the passage which should be opened out for discussion, and (ii) some general conclusions the group ought to reach as a result of the study. Here the questions which arise from 2 Timothy 3:16–17 should act as our guide.

3. The guidelines and questions which follow may help to provide a general framework for each discussion; leaders should use them as starting places which can be further developed. It is usually helpful to have a specific goal or theme in mind for group discussion, and one is suggested for each study. But even more important than tracing a single theme is understanding the teaching and the implications of the passage.

Leading the Group:

1. Announce the passage and theme for the study, and begin with prayer. In group studies it may be helpful to invite a different person to lead in prayer each time you meet.

2. Introduce the passage and theme, briefly reminding people of its outline and highlighting the content of each subsidiary section.

3. Lead the group through the discussion questions. Use your own if you are comfortable in doing so; those provided may be used, developing them with your own points. As discussion proceeds, continue to encourage the group first of all to discuss the significance of the passage (teaching) and only then its application (meaning for us). It may be helpful to write important points and applications on a board by way of summary as well as visual aid.

[137]

4. At the end of each meeting, remind members of the group of their assignments for the next meeting and encourage them to come prepared. Be sufficiently prepared as the leader to give specific assignments to individuals or even couples or groups to come with specific contributions ('John, would you try to find out something about the Judaisers for the next meeting?' 'Fiona, would you see what you can find out about the different ways in which 2 Corinthians 5:16 has been interpreted?').

5. Remember that you are the leader of the group! Encourage clear contributions, and do not be embarrassed to ask someone to explain what they have said more fully or to help them to do so ('Do you mean . . . ?').

Most groups include the 'over-talkative', the 'over-silent' and the 'red-herring raisers'! Leaders must control the first, encourage the second and redirect the third! Each leader will develop his or her own most natural way of doing that; but it will be helpful to think out what that is before the occasion arises! The first two groups can be helped by some judicious direction of questions to specific individuals or even groups (*e.g.*, 'How do those who are not working outside of the home apply this?' 'Jane, you know something about this from personal experience . . .'); the third by redirecting the discussion to the passage itself ('That is an interesting point, but isn't it true that this passage really concentrates on . . . ?'). It may be helpful to break the group up into smaller groups sometimes, giving each subgroup specific points to discuss and to report back on. A wise arranging of these smaller groups may also help each member to participate.

More important than any techniques we may develop is the help of the Spirit enabling us to understand and to apply the Scriptures. Have and encourage a humble, prayerful spirit.

6. Keep faith with the schedule; it is better that some of the group wished the study could have been longer than that others are inconvenienced by it stretching beyond the time limits set.

7. Close in prayer. As time permits, spend the closing minutes in corporate prayer, encouraging the group to apply what they have learned in praise and thanks, intercession and petition.

STUDY 1: 2 Corinthians 1:1–11

AIM: To recognise first how central God was to Paul's thinking, and to understand some of the purposes God may have in our troubles and suffering.

1. In what areas of life do we constantly need the renewal of God's grace?

2. How is the Bible's understanding of peace different from that of the world at large?

3. How would you answer someone who said, 'God is everyone's Father'? What does God's Fatherhood tell us about him?

4. Since the sufferings of our Lord Jesus for our salvation are unique, in what ways may we share in his sufferings?

5. What place may our sufferings have in our usefulness to others? How have we been encouraged by the experience of other people in times of difficulty? What examples can we give of this from the Bible itself?

6. What does it mean to 'set our hope' on God? How would you define hope, and specifically Christian hope?

7. If you were visiting Christians in difficulty and trouble, is this one of the first passages you might think of reading with them? What other passages might you use?

FOR STUDY 2: Read 2 Corinthians 1:12–2:4 and chapter 3.

STUDY 2: Corinthians 1:12–2:4

AIM: To grasp the importance of personal integrity if our lives are to demonstrate to the world how attractive the gospel of our Lord Jesus Christ is.

1. How do you think people in general would define integrity? Is Christian understanding of integrity any different?

2. In what kind of situations do you find your integrity under threat?

3. What are proper grounds for boasting in one another (v. 14)?

4. Can you think of promises God makes to keep us, to support us, to direct us, to provide for us, to deliver us, and to turn difficult and unpleasant things in our lives to good?

5. What constitutes a good conscience?

6. Can you think of situations where you have to choose between living according to worldly wisdom or according to God's grace (v. 12)? How do you make that choice?

7. What difference will it make to our lives if we live with 'the day of Christ' in view (v. 14)?

FOR STUDY 3: Read 2 Corinthians 2:5–3:6 and chapters 4 and 5.

STUDY 3: 2 Corinthians 2:5–3:6

AIM: To appreciate the necessity for the careful and sensitive exercise of church discipline; to encourage us to see ourselves as servants of the gospel, and to recognise the expected evidences of this.

1. How would you answer those who suggest that church discipline is an intrusion upon, and a violation of, an individual's freedom?

2. What are the purposes of church discipline?

3. What does it mean to forgive as we have been forgiven, and to do so 'in the presence of Christ' (v. 10)?

4. How does God open doors for us to share and preach the gospel?

5. Without naming them, can you identity Christian believers whose lives bear the fragrance of the Lord Jesus? What marks them out?

6. What bitter experiences in a Christian's life – like the crushing of a fruit or kernel – may yield a special fragrance of Christ?

7. If you were listening to an evangelist – perhaps with a view to inviting him to assist your church – what would you look for in his message, character and reputation?

FOR STUDY 4: Read 2 Corinthians 3:7–18 and chapter 6.

STUDY 4: 2 Corinthians 3:7–18

AIM: To remind ourselves of the inestimable privilege of living under God's new covenant rather than the old.

1. In what ways do the Ten Commandments reflect and reveal God's character?

2. How does God use his law to bring us to Christ? Or, to change the picture, how does God use the needle of the law to make way for the thread of the gospel?

3. How important is the teaching of the Ten Commandments, first, to Christians, and secondly, to unbelievers?

4. Our prayers as believers should be marked by both reverence and boldness. Is there any potential conflict between the two? Justify your answers.

5. What help does this passage give us in our praying for the Jewish people?

6. What lessons may we learn about the work of the Holy Spirit in this passage?

7. How does God achieve in us an increasing likeness to the Lord Jesus?

FOR STUDY 5: Read 2 Corinthians 4:1–5:10 and chapters 7 and 8.

STUDY 5: 2 Corinthians 4:1–5:10

AIM: To recognise common causes of discouragement as we fulfil our commission, and, at the same time, to recognise that they provide no grounds for giving up; to recognise also the great stimulus to obedience and Christ-glorifying service that the assurance of our future as believers gives.

1. What are the discouragements you meet as you try to share the gospel of the Lord Jesus with others?

2. How would you answer someone who asks, 'There are so many religions today, and different Christian groups, how can you be sure that what you say is the truth?'

3. What lessons may we learn from Paul's description of us as 'jars of clay' (4:7)

4. How important is encouragement in the Christian life? How may we give it to one another?

5. Why is heaven such an attractive prospect for the Christian? Give biblical reasons for your answers.

6. What are the evidences of God's Spirit living within us?

7. What place do ambitions and goals have in the Christian life? What makes them different from the ambitions and goals of those who are not Christians?

FOR STUDY 6: Read 2 Corinthians 5:11–6:13 and chapters 9 and 10.

STUDY 6: 2 Corinthians 5:11–6:13

AIM: To recognise the fundamental nature of our responsibility for evangelism, and the methods and motives that are to govern us.

1. How would you convey in contemporary language the message of reconciliation to a non-Christian?

2. The 'no longer' element about the Christian life is all part of our being a 'new creation' (v. 17). What radical changes have occurred in your life as a result of new birth?

3. What makes the death of the Lord Jesus Christ different from all other deaths?

4. While all Christians have responsibility for sharing the good news, those called to preach have special responsibility. In the light of this passage, how should we pray for them in this task?

5. How may people's outward appearance or circumstances influence whether or not we seek to share the gospel with them? Are there people or groups we consider impossible? Why is such an attitude wrong?

6. In what ways can the ministry of the gospel be discredited?

7. Why is endurance so important in the Christian life? If answers do not readily come, look up Matthew 10:22; Mark 13:13; Acts 14:22; 1 Peter 1:6–7; Revelation 2:26.

FOR STUDY 7: Read 2 Corinthians 6:14–7:16 and chapters 11 and 12.

STUDY 7: 2 Corinthians 6:14–7:16

AIM: To understand our proper separation to God in the world.

1. What do we mean when we say that we no longer belong to the world as once we did?

2. How would you answer someone who asks, 'Why should a Christian not marry someone who is not a Christian?'

3. What are the likely tension points if a Christian is in a business partnership with someone who does not share faith in the Lord Jesus Christ? What biblical principles should guide us here?

4. What are the practical consequences of believers constituting God's Temple in which he chooses to dwell?

5. What are common causes of misunderstandings in human relationships?

6. Why is it better to deal with difficulties face to face than to put what we feel in writing?

7. There is a *godly* sorrow for sin and a *worldly* sorrow. How may we distinguish the two?

FOR STUDY 8: Read 2 Corinthians 8:1–15 and chapter 13.

STUDY 8: 2 Corinthians 8:1–15

AIM: To show the inevitable link between grace and generosity, in that generous giving on our part is a proper response to God's grace.

1. Illustrate from the Bible itself, and then from your own experience, that God is the giving God.

2. What may we see as the significance of the fact that grace and gratitude are translated from the same Greek word in the New Testament?

3. In what practical ways may our giving be part of our Christian service?

4. When have you been most stirred or prompted to give beyond what might have been expected of you? What do you learn from this about giving?

5. In what ways did our Lord become poor for our sakes?

6. How has our Lord Jesus' poverty made us rich?

7. What lessons may we learn from the scripture Paul quotes in verse 15?

FOR STUDY 9: Read 2 Corinthians 8:16–9:15 and chapters 14 and 15.

STUDY 9: 2 Corinthians 8:16–9:15

AIM: To recognise the importance of handling money carefully, so that our actions are beyond criticism and honour God.

1. The churches chose Titus' two companions to be their representatives (vv. 18–19, 23). What does that tell us about the corporate life of the early churches and their relationship?

2. In choosing people to administer the finances of the local church, for what qualities should we look?

3. What place does example have in the Christian life? Can you think of areas where the example of another Christian or group of Christians has stimulated you to action?

4. The New Testament frequently calls upon us to 'remember', as in 9:6. Can you think of other calls to stir our memory? If not, consider Exodus 20:8; Psalm 77:11; 105:5; Ecclesiastes 12:1; Luke 17:32; John 15:20; Ephesians 2:11–12; 2 Timothy 2:8; Hebrews 13:3, 7, and especially 1 Corinthians 11:24–25.

5. 'God loves a cheerful giver' (v. 7). What does this tell us about God? What are the implications of this and our experience of new birth?

6. Paul writes in verse 11 of God making us 'enriched in every way'. In what ways other than financial may God make us rich?

7. Who among God's people should be the particular focus of our giving (v. 12)?

FOR STUDY 10: Read 2 Corinthians 10:1–18 and chapter 16.

STUDY 10: 2 Corinthians 10:1–18

AIM: To recognise the way in which we should respond to criticism and false accusations, avoiding the snare of judging others.

1. When we are the target of false accusations or insinuations, when is it wise to say nothing, and when is it right to respond?

2. How would you illustrate from the gospels the meekness and gentleness of our Lord Jesus Christ?

3. How important are meekness and gentleness for good relationships within the church?

4. We have suggested that Satan delights in our going to extremes. Can you think of examples?

5. What are the evidences the Bible says we should look for in our lives as proof of new birth?

6. Why is it foolish to classify or compare ourselves with others?

7. How real a peril is boasting? How may we best cure ourselves of it?

FOR STUDY 11: Read 2 Corinthians 11:1–15 and chapter 17.

STUDY 11: 2 Corinthians 11:1–15

AIM: To recognise the spiritual battle in which we are engaged and the areas of life in which we need to be watchful.

1. What makes jealousy 'divine' jealousy (v. 2)?

2. What does Paul's description of his concern for the Corinthians in verse 2 teach us about pastoral work?

3. What may we learn from this passage about the ways in which Satan often works?

4. What are the greatest threats to our devotion to the Lord Jesus?

5. What do we find most helpful in maintaining our love for the Lord Jesus?

6. Can you think of occasions when you have been aware of people preaching a different Jesus, or different gospel, or displaying a different spirit? What alerted you to the differences?

7. Discuss the relevance and application of 1 Thessalonians 5:21 in the light of this passage.

FOR STUDY 12: Read 2 Corinthians 11:16–12:13 and chapters 18 and 19.

STUDY 12: 2 Corinthians 11:16:12:13

AIM: To recognise the folly of engaging in any kind of boasting about either ourselves or our service for God.

1. Can you think of contemporary examples of false teaching? If so, how far do its characteristics match those of the false teaching Paul describes (v. 20)?

2. When are we most tempted to boast? What practical actions can we take to avoid the danger?

3. When we serve others, how may we ensure that we do not attach people to ourselves, but rather to the Lord Jesus Christ?

4. If someone claims a special spiritual experience, or if we ourselves do, how may its genuineness be tested?

5. Why is spiritual pride worse than many other forms of pride?

6. How may Satan often try to make capital out of illness and our physical difficulties?

7. Explore the theme of weakness in Paul's letters to the Corinthians (*e.g.*, *1 Cor.* 1:26–31; 4:10; 9:22; *2 Cor.* 11:29–30; 12:9–10; 13:9). What may we learn from Paul's experience?

FOR STUDY 13: Read 2 Corinthians 12:14–13:14 and chapter 20.

STUDY 13: 2 Corinthians 12:14–13:14

AIM: To identify the purposes Paul had in view for his intended visit to Corinthians, and to learn from them.

1. Can you think of situations in which doing the right thing has been misunderstood? As you reflect upon these situations, should you have acted differently?

2. How right is it not to want to be a burden to people?

3. What may we learn about our responsibility towards those whom we are privileged to point to faith in our Lord Jesus Christ (12:14–16)?

4. We cannot avoid sometimes being misunderstood or misrepresented. When should we defend ourselves, and when should we not?

5. Since sexual sin and indecent behaviour arise from impurity of thought, how may we help ourselves protect the purity of our minds?

6. When we examine ourselves, what should we use to help us? What kinds of questions should we ask ourselves?

7. The final paragraph of our study of this passage focuses upon 2 Corinthians 13:14. Explore the suggested blessings we pray for when we take these words upon our lips.

FOR FURTHER READING

The following books are recommended for study of Paul's Second Letter to the Corinthians:

Paul Barnett: *The Message of 2 Corinthians*, Inter-Varsity Press, 1988

Charles Hodge: *1 & 2 Corinthians*, Banner of Truth Trust, Edinburgh, 1974

Colin Kruse: *2 Corinthians*, Inter-Varsity Press, Leicester, 1987

Geoffrey Wilson: *New Testament Commentaries, Volume 1: Romans to Ephesians*, Banner of Truth Trust, Edinburgh, 2005